# EDUCATING THE INQUIRING MIND

## THE CHALLENGE FOR SCHOOL SCIENCE

### GUY CLAXTON
*King's College London*

## HARVESTER
## WHEATSHEAF

NEW YORK  LONDON  TORONTO  SYDNEY  TOKYO  SINGAPORE

First published 1991 by
Harvester Wheatsheaf,
66 Wood Lane End, Hemel Hempstead,
Hertfordshire, HP2 4RG
A division of Simon & Schuster International Group

Typeset in 10 on 12 pt Bembo by Pentacor plc
Printed and bound in Great Britain by
BPCC Wheatons Ltd

British Library Cataloguing in Publication Data

Claxton, Guy
Educating the inquiring mind: The challenge for
school science.
I.Title
507

ISBN 0-7450-0979-4
ISBN 0-7450-0980-8 pbk

1 2 3 4 5 95 94 93 92 91

# CONTENTS

# PREFACE

For the last 11 years, since joining the staff of the Chelsea College Centre for Science and Mathematics Education at the University of London, I have been concerned, in one way or another, with the state of science education in secondary schools. Largely this has been from the point of view of a psychologist with an abiding interest in the processes of learning. The learning of science offers some particular challenges because its obvious difficulty, at least for a considerable number of adolescents, is amenable to explanation in so many different ways. Is it just intrinsically hard? Do some children simply lack the brain power to cope with it? Do students' own half-baked ideas about scientific phenomena get in the way of learning the 'truth'? Maybe the problem is motivational rather than cognitive: science is just boring to many young people. Perhaps the essential 'maleness' of science puts off girls – and a number of boys too. And so on. It is indeed a fascinating puzzle, and over the years I contributed to the debate a trickle of conference presentations, articles (both published and more usually unpublished), book chapters and book reviews, and talks to various professional bodies of both teachers and scientists. Science education is one of a hundred comfortable sub-professions within the study of education as a whole, and I camped, from time to time, on its outskirts.

This book arose out of the growing realisation that we do not have a problem with science education; we have a disaster with it. Reading the literature, talking to teachers and students, and sitting in lessons, usually in the role of tutor to trainee secondary science teachers, it became obvious that what was being offered missed the mark of what the majority of students needed and wanted to know, not just by a bit but by a mile. Much well-intentioned, thoughtful and expensive curriculum innovation seemed, time and again, to end up on the scrap-heap of good ideas that never quite took off, leaving science teachers, only too aware of the narrowness of the band of what they could count as their successes, more confused than ever. The interest in a chewy little psychological problem began to give way to a much more urgent concern with the whole state of things: with what it was that young people really needed to get from their science education; with the apparent grandiosity, and sometimes incoherence, of the espoused aims of science educators; with the naivety of some of the images of science itself that were embedded within teaching styles and topics; with the more general educational values that seemed to lie behind different approaches to the science curriculum. Despite much real concern with 'relevance' and 'skills' over the last 20 years and more, why was there such a strong air of '*plus ça change, plus c'est la même chose*'?

If war is too important to be left to the generals, my feeling is that preparing young people to live as effectively as possible in a world saturated with the creatures, and monsters, of science is too important an issue to be merely the preserve of experts in science education. I am very far from being such an expert, and I hope that those who are, many of them my colleagues and friends over the years, will forgive my presumption, and I am sure, frequent naivety, as I venture into their territory. Though what I have to say is uncompromising, and some of it will sound to them old hat, I intend this book to be a small but thoroughly positive contribution to what we all agree is a vitally urgent and important debate.

Partly I have covered old ground, and written in as lucid and lively a style as I can muster, because my audience is broader than the experts. I want to speak to scientists themselves, and to parents, many of whom are profoundly worried about the lack of scientific confidence and competence they see in young people. I want especially to speak to teachers, most of whom simply do not have time to plough through academic books. I am convinced that the only changes in education that stand a chance of being both radical and real (as opposed to rhetorical) are those that are generated by teachers themselves; ideas that are tried out, talked about, and which respond to the frustrations and aspirations that teachers are actually experiencing. An ounce of such grass-roots innovation is worth more than a ton of imposed bureaucratic change. I hope that what I say will be accessible to teachers and will help them think.

This is not a recipe book, however: anyone looking for another prescription, to be taken three times a day before lessons, will be disappointed. I do not intend, nor am I equipped, to offer specific practical help in lesson planning. I want to contribute at a different level. The solutions that people come up with reflect and embody their own tacit analysis of the problem, and their implicit understandings of what it is possible and desirable to do. My intention, in as friendly a way as possible, is to bring some of these presuppositions into the light and to put them up for grabs, so that the debate is well-informed, and so that areas of fatalistic or wishful thinking do not slip through. So overburdened practitioners will not find here any more than the most tentative sketches of answers. What I hope is that they might find some clearer – and in some ways tougher – questions.

I would like to thank here some of the colleagues and students who tolerated, supported and challenged my own developing thinking. At the Chelsea Centre for Science and Mathematics Education, and later the King's College Centre for Educational Studies, there were Philip Adey, Paul Black, Joan Bliss, Bob Fairbrother, Wynne Harlen, John Head, Arthur Lucas, Tony Mansell, John May, Martin Monk, Patricia Murphy, Jon Ogborn, Terry Russell, Neil Ryder and Joan Solomon. Michael Shayer, my 'A' level chemistry teacher and later colleague at Chelsea, was probably the first person to get me thinking about the learning of science (and also incidentally about the potential for the combination of poetry and jazz). Elsewhere in the United Kingdom I've had interesting conversations with Rosalind Driver, John Gilbert, Clive Sutton and Mike Watts.

Over the last few years I have frequently enjoyed the hospitality and support of members of the Science Education Research Unit, now the Centre for Science and Mathematics Education Research, at the University of Waikato, New Zealand: Miles Barker, Andy Begg, Beverley Bell, Fred Biddulph, Malcolm Carr, Mark Cosgrove, John Faire, Mary Faire, Teresa Fernandez, Anne Hume, Alister Jones, Chris Kirk, Valda Kirkwood, Kala Lal, Jane McChesney, John Pearson, Jan Sylvester and Ian Torrey. Special thanks to Beverley for all her help with my visits, and for starting off the Kiwi connection by introducing my papers to Roger Osborne, who first invited me to Waikato, and then was tragically killed in a car accident before we could meet. And to Malcolm and his family for their love and support.

I have also valued conversations with Peter Fensham, Dick Gunstone, Leo West and Dick White from Monash, Leon Pines from the USA and Gaalen Erickson from Canada.

Several people read the manuscript for me in draft, and made very valuable suggestions: Miles Barker, Colin Blakemore, Robert Bolick of Harvester Wheatsheaf, Justin Dillon and Jeremy Frank. Some of the publisher's reviews were very kind and helpful. These people, known and anonymous, are of course to blame for any errors or silliness they allowed to pass unchecked; while all their insights I have shamelessly dissolved in the text, hoping to pass them off as my own.

Guy Claxton
*King's College London*

# CHAPTER ONE

———————— • ————————

## SCIENCE FOR ALL?

Where the young child, at least until his thinking has been spoiled by adults, has a great advantage is in situations – and many, even most, real-life situations are like this – where there is so much seemingly senseless data that it is impossible to tell what questions to ask. He is much better at taking in this kind of data; he is better able to tolerate its confusion; and he is much better at picking out the patterns, hearing the faint signal amid all the noise. Above all, he is much less likely than adults to make hard and fast conclusions on the basis of too little data, or having made such conclusions, to refuse to consider any new data that does not support them. And these are the vital skills of thought which, in our hurry to get him thinking in the way we do, we may very well stunt or destroy in the process of 'educating' him.

John Holt

Everyone seems to agree that it is important for today's young people to know something of the world of science, and that it is the job of school to try to make sure that this happens. We live, so the argument goes, in a technological world, where our every move is channelled and influenced by the products of science. You cannot be born these days, in the industrialised world, without the aid of science, nor can you die. From machines that can keep scraps of life alive, and nappies that magic their contents away, to drugs for Alzheimer's disease, and even the canned music in the undertaker's waiting room, our needs and interests are aroused, directed and satisfied by the appliances of science. Open the paper – a hi-tech product now if ever there was one – and you will read daily about genetic fingerprinting, computer fraud, factory-farming, and drug tests on athletes; turn on the television, whose picture is the tip of a giant iceberg of sophisticated physics, and you will be bombarded with advertisements for margarines that are 'polyunsaturated', washing powders that use 'enzymes' and cars that have 'catalytic converters'.

If one is not to feel helpless in a world that is 'polysaturated' with science, its creations and its lingo, one must have at least a rudimentary grasp of what it is all about. Nobody could be expected, these days, to be capable of fixing their TV, microwave, home computer or even the car that was 'hand-built by robots'. But if one knows enough to be able to talk to the experts, and is confident enough to insist that they explain what is wrong, and what they intend to do about it, then one has a big advantage. This is perhaps most essential in the medical sphere, where we need to know enough to make sensible choices about our own health, based on the information that doctors can provide. But a sense of control in many areas of life depends on some familiarity with technology and the principles on which it rests. Even consumer magazines such as 'Which?' need a bit of scientific nous to understand the purpose and meaning of the tests which they report. And it is almost a necessity nowadays to be able to provide some 'consumer protection' for oneself. It is important to know – or better, to be able to find out – whether it is really true that artificial preservatives, 'E numbers' and aluminium frying-pans are bad for your health, under what circumstances, and why. It is useful to be able to tell whether the gizmo on the central heating radiators that costs an extra thirty pounds is really going to pay for itself, or is just a gimmick.

Not only should we be able to interact, up to a point, with the products of science; we should have some grasp of its dangers and limitations, so that we can hold informed opinions about science-related issues. People ought to be able to ask pointed questions about the necessity for experimentation on live animals; about the reasons why cars last for such a short time; about the costs and risks of nuclear power; about the 'greenhouse effect' and 'ozone holes'; about the arguments that the big pharmaceutical companies use for charging ten times as much for branded drugs as for their 'generic' equivalents; and so on. Again, if people are to have some sense of control over such matters, then they need to be able to formulate good questions and to detect bad answers. Even if one is not quite capable of building one's own cyclotron in the back garden, one ought to be able to speak 'pidgin science-ese', to know when someone is trying to blind you with science, and to have enough of a basic understanding of the world of science to take, for either practical or recreational reasons, an intelligent interest in what scientists have to say.

Behind the findings and the language of science, there lie the more general impressions and beliefs that people hold about the nature and status of scientific knowledge, and what it is that scientists actually are, and do. To engage with the science that they meet, people need some sense of the kind of enterprise that science is, and realistic expectations about what it can, and cannot, provide. Individuals and societies will lose out if they have either an exaggerated reverence, or a blanket hostility, towards the scientific world. We cannot get away with blaming the scientists for the short-sighted exploitation of non-renewable natural resources, nor for the pollution we read about or breathe in every day. The technology we have produced is a mirror of our *non*-scientific values, habits and needs. If thousands of us ordinary people were not so wasteful with water, there would be less pollution in the rivers. If we were not so concerned with our appearances, there would be no rabbits with painful gunk stuck in their eyes. It is too easy, and unfair, to scapegoat the 'scientists'. Yet neither are they exempt from the requirement to think about the values that underlie what they do. It may not be a good enough defence to say that one designed a complicated new surgical technique, or altered the genes in a living animal, just because it was an interesting challenge to try. Everyone needs the ability and the inclination to be vigilant about the costs and risks that scientific advances may bring with them.

So an accurate appreciation of science is needed by potential science producers as well as by all of us who are science consumers. However 'green' one's views of national or global economics, a ready supply of good scientists is going to be as much a necessity in the future as it has become today. People's definition of 'good' might vary somewhat, but we are certainly not going to be able to feed the world, or clean it up, by a return to pre-scientific attitudes and practices. The values and priorities of science may very well have to change, but the need for scientific expertise will certainly remain. Soft technologies are by no means always easy technologies to design, and the scientific problems involved in deriving useable and sizeable amounts of energy from the sun, the wind or the waves are formidable; while on a more conventional level, national prosperities are heavily dependent on both technology and on an investment in so-called 'pure' research. It was a resident not of an Ivory Tower, but of Number 10 Downing Street who said in 1988:

> It is mainly by unlocking nature's most basic secrets, whether it be about the structure of matter and the fundamental forces or about the nature of life itself, that we have been able to build the modern world. Although basic science can have colossal economic rewards, they are totally unpredictable. And therefore the rewards cannot be judged by immediate results. . .Indeed it is astonishing how quickly the benefits of curiosity-driven research sometimes appear. The natural desire of gifted people to excel and gain the credit for their work must be harnessed.[1]

But if societies need scientists, they need people who want to *become* scientists, and this means that sizeable numbers of them must acquire a more-or-less accurate and positive image of scientific work, as well as the beginnings of some scientific understanding, when they are young. They need to be given a feel for what scientific research involves, and the range of different kinds of science – from living with gorillas in African mountains, to synthesising new kinds of food preservative – that they might like to earn their living by carrying out. They will need some kind of a taste of what the rewards and satisfactions are, as well as some of the ethical and practical problems involved, in the real business of 'doing science'.

In addition to these public reasons why education in science is important, there is also a widespread feeling that the kind of thinking and learning that Science (with a capital S) requires is of potential value to everyone in their daily lives, regardless of whether they are formally tackling a 'scientific' problem or not. Some sort of training in science, so the argument goes, equips people with attitudes and skills which will stand them in good stead, whatever career or lifestyle they decide to take up. They will be able to observe more carefully and think more clearly, and such abilities will be capable of being deployed across a much broader range of informal and real-life problems than those that are scientific only in the technical sense. Deciding with your partner what kind of contraception to use, or trying your hand at do-it-yourself surveying when buying a house, are examples of real-world problems that might be assisted by some scientific type of reasoning, as well as a smattering of accurate scientific knowledge, even though they *also* involve other kinds of thinking and reflecting as well.

So there are many compelling reasons why science education is important. It matters in terms of economic performance. It matters in terms of the search for better ways of exploring the potential of nature, without damaging it and choking the planet. It matters in terms of people's ability to engage with the world of science for pleasure and entertainment. It matters because people need to feel some control over the selection and maintenance of the technology that they make use of in their lives. It matters because they ought to be able to take part in some of the crucial science-related debates with which our societies are faced. It matters because stereotypes of science and scientists, whether favourable or unfavourable, distort people's contributions to such debates. It matters because it seems to offer people a powerful kind of thinking tool to be used in making decisions and solving problems in their own lives. And it matters because science constitutes a major and constantly changing part of our culture and without some understanding of its rudiments people cannot, as C.P. Snow said many years ago, be considered properly educated at all.

With such an array of arguments behind one, it is hard to imagine anyone, whatever their politics, values or circumstances, who would deny that some form of education in and about science must form part of a general attempt to equip young people to cope as well as they can with a complicated world. Science education deserves a central place in the curriculum. And that indeed is what it is coming to occupy throughout the world. Many countries, driven as much by concerns of national prosperity and the need to compete in technologically dominated international markets as by sympathy for the plight of the bemused individual, are busy promoting science within the school syllabus. The National Curriculum for England and Wales, for example, has now enshrined science as one of the three 'core subjects' of the school curriculum, compulsory for all up to the age of 16, and occupying, along with mathematics and English, the lion's share of the timetable. The specification of the seventeen 'attainment targets' in science contains a detailed prescription of what all young people are supposed to know, or be able to do, by the time they leave school, from the simple ('list and collate observations') to the advanced ('explain electrolysis in terms of ionic reactions'). Australia, New Zealand and the USA too, have recently been busy inspecting and revising their school syllabuses in science. And many of the so-called developing or unindustrialised countries, which have largely identified development with scientific progress, consider it a national priority to send teachers on expensive overseas courses, in order to pick up the latest ideas about how to teach science from those who are supposed to know. Clearly governments and educators the world over see the value of science education, and are willing to commit substantial amounts of money to it, and to require school students to spend large amounts of time studying it.

### THE PRESENT SITUATION

Despite these commitments there remain grave misgivings about the success of science education programmes, however. The return on these national investments looks disappointing whichever of the general aims which we sketched above is considered. From the economic point of view, it appears that not enough young people are emerging from the schools good enough and keen enough to meet the needs of scientifically-based industry. There is a growing shortage of science graduates in Britain – a 7.5 per cent shortfall in the summer of 1988 according to the Committee of Vice-Chancellors and Principals, the national forum for those who run the universities.[2] In the same year the pharmaceutical company Beecham claims that it managed to recruit only 70 of the 120 graduate scientists it wanted; Wellcome said it would have to recruit science graduates from Europe; and Glaxo substantially raised its starting salaries to try to attract fresh graduates.

A report to the British Prime Minister by the Advisory Council for Science and Technology in 1990 warned of the shortage of skilled scientists in the internationally competitive field of biotechnology, and expressed concern yet again about the 'brain-drain'. The council's worries were given an added piquancy when the press conference at which the report was announced was told that one of its principal authors was unable to be present as he had recently emigrated to run a biotechnology company in California.[3] In terms of their ability to produce young people who like science enough to want to make their living at it, and who have learnt enough to do so, schools do not seem to be as successful as the captains of industry would like.

This seems to reflect both a failure to turn young people on to science, and a failure to give them an adequate grounding even in the most straightforward scientific knowledge and skills. Years of school science seem often to leave little impression on the minds of large numbers of students. The Assessment of Performance Unit, set up and funded at considerable expense by the British Government's Department of Education and Science (note the linking of the two words even here) to monitor the achievements of science students at different ages, reported their findings for 15-year-olds in 1988.[4] They found that 80–90 per cent did not read a simple water manometer (basically the height of a column of water in a glass tube) correctly; 45 per cent did not read a pre-set value on a stop-clock correctly; 80 per cent did not weigh a given mass of water correctly; 86 per cent did not use correctly a measuring cylinder to find out the volume of water in a cup; and 50 per cent did not even read a set value on a ruler correctly.

In other words after at least four years of studying science and doing hundreds of experiments, well over half of the 15-year-olds appeared incapable of using the most basic measuring instruments of the science laboratory in a proper manner. I say 'appeared' because I simply do not believe that they were actually unable to exercise or master these trivially simple skills correctly. After all, we are talking about young people the vast majority of whom are at least as capable as their teachers and parents of setting video recorders, reading clinical thermometers, programming microwave ovens and weighing out flour.

Concern about such a pitiful return for so much hard work has led over the last two or three decades to an almost continual attempt to devise better teaching schemes and approaches. However, to suppose that a problem of such magnitude can be solved by some fine tuning of teaching technique, or rejigging of the syllabus, which will enable these operations to be 'acquired' more successfully, may well be to construe the problem within too narrow a framework. Are we really looking at a situation where young people are applying their cognitive resources as best they can, but are being defeated by the sheer difficulty of the demands that are being placed upon them? Could it not be instead that some, maybe many, of them are so bamboozled by the whole enterprise that they have more or less switched off, and are firing on a vastly reduced number of mental cylinders?[5]

If we are not being very successful at producing the skills and attitudes of real science, are we not at least sending out young people who have a fair smattering of knowledge about the natural world, and the general, powerful ideas that scientists have come up with? Unfortunately not. Not only do science lessons fail to teach reliably the rudiments of laboratory procedure; they even seem to fail to transmit the most basic of scientific facts. Two recent surveys of the public's scientific knowledge, one in Britain and one in the USA, revealed a phenomenal level of ignorance. Well under half of the American public, and only a third of the British, know that the earth revolves round the sun once a year. A third of both British and Americans think that radioactive milk could be made safe by boiling it. Most of those surveyed think that antibiotics kill viruses. While, as one of the researchers says, 'there is a growing recognition in the industrialised world that scientific literacy is an important component of long-term economic growth and effective citizenship', he is forced to conclude from these surveys that 'in two of the world's oldest and most prominent democracies at least nine out of ten citizens lack the scientific literacy to understand and participate in the formulation of public policy on a very important segment of their national policy agendas'.[6] Contrast these results with those of a series of other surveys commissioned for the Economic and Social Science Research Council, – showing that when people see a personal or practical use for science, and are sufficiently motivated, they frequently show a remarkable capacity to learn and retain scientific data – and the explanations in terms of the intrinsic difficulty of science begin to look even more thin.[7]

If the basic facts of school science do not 'stick', we cannot be too hopeful about the theories. And indeed there is recent research showing that the major effect of attendance at science lessons between the ages of 11 and 16 is to enable students to express more fluently precisely the same misunderstandings which they had when they started.[8] Scratch physics undergraduates, even, and you will likely find that they *intuitively* think about such a fundamental notion as 'force' in just the same way as they did at primary school – a way which is quite 'wrong' from the scientists' point of view.[9] It appears that once you entice even successful students (and their teachers) off the well-trodden path of textbook definitions, standard demonstrations and worked examples, their surface layer of formal scientific understanding breaks up very quickly, revealing itself to have been at best only skin deep. Underneath there remain lay theories, curious mixtures of personal experience and dubious common sense, which seem to have persisted quite unaltered by the lick of scientific sophistication which had overlain them.

And what of the intention to develop the skills and habits of sound thinking? Despite many claims that science education is potentially able to bring people on as rational thinkers, there is no evidence for it. Research on formal reasoning skills has shown no difference between arts and science students, even up to the graduate level.[10] And overall school seems to be a very inefficient inducer of rationality. A large-scale survey in America recently has shown that the quality of the arguments that people use in their informal, everyday conversations is scarcely related at all to the amount of education they have received.[11] If the education we have is to be assessed on its ability to develop sound thinking, then it offers a very small return indeed on an enormous investment of young people's time.

## THE RECENT HISTORY OF SCIENCE EDUCATION

The present dissatisfaction with education in science is nothing new. Fairly regularly for the last forty years or more people have become worried about the lack of enjoyment and achievement that many students derive from science lessons. One way and another, curriculum developers have tried to find ways of escaping from the model of science as a body of certain knowledge, discovered by clever, distant people, which it is important for students to master – i.e. to retain and be able to manipulate in some well-channelled ways. This view of science teaching as the transmission of a remote, incontrovertible, and (for nearly all personal purposes) useless collection of facts and theories, larded with periodic experimental 'demonstrations', has often been held to be the reason behind many students' experience of science as hard and boring. The search was therefore on to find ways of making it more 'accessible' and 'relevant', especially for the majority of students who lacked the ability, or perhaps the inclination, to plough on towards specialised study or a degree in one of the science subjects.

This search has frequently come to focus on the possibility of using the activities of science, rather than its products, as the primary topic of teaching and learning. Although the curriculum obviously has to provide some things to find out *about*, people have tried in many ways to shift the emphasis away from learning (in the sense of 'retaining') scientific facts and theories, towards the benefit to be gained from exercising the process of 'finding out' itself. The scientific method, so-called, has been analysed into a variety of component skills, mental and perceptual as well as practical, and the plan has been to use study and experiment on some scientific topics to develop these skills.

Time and again the idea has kept emerging that science education would be improved if students could behave more like scientists themselves, and that if they were allowed and encouraged to do so, they would be able to acquire some of the subject matter more easily and more enjoyably. A recent American book for example, reasserts this principle strongly. 'The best way for students to acquire the rich conceptual structure of scientific knowledge is by engaging in those very processes that created it.'[12] And people in the field are fond of quoting a Chinese proverb which says: 'I hear, and I forget. I see, and I remember. I do, and I understand.'[13] So the

1960s saw the introduction of courses such as Nuffield Science in Britain or Chemstudy in the USA, which placed a much higher premium than previously on experimental work, and the processes of discovery, and these were supposed to produce a school population which was more 'science minded'.

While such changes often seemed to benefit those students who were already doing reasonably well in science, and who were likely to be on track for higher study and possible careers in science, they have so far been a thorough disappointment as far as the involvement and learning of the other 70–80 per cent of the young secondary school population are concerned – precisely the group that was giving most cause for concern.[14] Though there is disagreement about the cause, there is little doubt that the involvement of students in practical activity does not of itself lead to greater understanding of, or enthusiasm for, science. Certainly the weight of the *content* seems, despite everybody's best intentions, to keep crushing the avowed concern with the *process*, perhaps because science teachers themselves have rarely felt quite confident enough to maintain the desired shift of priorities in practice. The processes themselves, often described as 'the skill of observation', or 'the ability to test hypotheses', almost always turn out in practice to boil down to the familiar, specialised laboratory techniques of measurement and experimentation, and therefore to remain remote from real life. And despite the theoretically positive, but practically disappointing,[15] changes incorporated in the GCSE (the new national 16+ examination in England and Wales), an examination system that, in the end, awards marks more for retention than investigation is going to drive the attention of both teachers and students back to the textbook answers.

SCIENCE IN EVERYDAY LIFE

Out of the interest in the process skills of science has grown the more ambitious idea that I alluded to in the Introduction to this chapter: that these skills and capabilities might not be applicable only to the laboratory world of formal scientific research, but could have utility more generally in the world of everyday learning, problem solving and decision making. If this were so, then we might be able to devise a form of science education that was of real, practical help to *all* young people, and not just to the 'elite' minority who were heading off for further study and training in Science with a capital S. Somehow we might be able to use the knowledge and techniques of Science to foster the development of more general-purpose ways of thinking about problems and testing out ideas – a scientific (with a small 's' now) frame of mind that would be of value to all.

Aims for science education have begun to emerge which are couched in terms like 'helping students make sense of their world', 'developing their ability to be effective learners', 'developing real-life problem-solving skills', or 'training sound thinking'. Such slogans point to an opportunity, but they do not on their own, of course, tell us how to make it a reality – or even whether it is actually achievable. For that, much further thought is needed, particularly in three areas. First, we need to discover whether there really is such a thing as 'scientific thinking' and if so what it consists of. Second, we shall have to define the raw material that students bring with them – the pre-existing stock of informal learning abilities, and the everyday understandings, which are to be refined by science education into the sharper, more analytical, tools of science. And third, we must investigate what kinds of real-life predicament are amenable to scientific thinking, and how they can be identified.

Research over the last decade has begun to focus on some of these crucial questions, in an attempt to uncover why the generally applauded move towards the process view of science education turns out to be so hard to make work. In the late 1970s researchers began to take a closer look at the realities of science lessons, and of the minds of science learners – the ideas and abilities that they were bringing with them into the laboratory. And the 1980s saw the publication, in forms that were designed to be accessible to science teachers and others who are not experts in the ins and outs of educational research, of many of the findings from these endeavours. In England there has been Rosalind Driver's *The Pupil As Scientist*, in Australia Richard White's *Learning Science*, in New Zealand Roger Osborne and Peter Freyberg's *Learning in Science*, and in the USA Joseph Novak and Bob Gowin's *Learning how to Learn*, which focused, like the others, on the special processes and problems of learning that students encountered in studying science.[16]

These studies revealed just how important, and how extensive, young people's ideas are about a host of scientific topics. Much is now known about the kinds of intuitions, for example, that young people of various ages can be expected to have about life or gravity or electricity or light, and about the ways in which these pre-existing ideas provide an indigenous mental culture that resists, sometimes quite strongly, the introduction of the 'better' ideas of formal science. Better they may be, in scientific terms; but students do not commonly experience the urgent dissatisfaction with their own half-baked notions which would induce them to undertake the difficult job of getting their brains round the hard-edged, unfamiliar concepts of physics, chemistry and biology – despite these concepts being touted as having profound value and importance.

Out of this strand of research has come the call for teachers to make contact with these intuitive, personal theories, and to devise ways of getting students to bring them to mind and to enter them in an experimental competition against the scientists' view. Yet very often these well-intentioned overtures give way all too rapidly to the persistent concern with 'getting the stuff across', and they turn out in practice to embody not a new set of priorities for science education but an increasingly transparent attempt to ease the assimilation of the same old rota of venerable abstractions. The motivational spark still obstinately refuses, for many students, to jump the gap and ignite their own enthusiasm.

## SCIENTISTS' SCIENCE

The idea that science education ought to show students something of the real world of science, and give them at least a taste of what being a scientist is like, has led over the last few years to an increasing interest in the complicated reality of scientific research, as opposed to the smooth and simplified face that it has tended to present. An interest by science educators in the history, philosophy and sociology of science has revealed that the *image* of scientific activity which has traditionally been conveyed by school science is in many ways false. Presenting research as a purely rational process of hypothesis-testing, for example, in which, as Thomas Huxley is reputed to have said, 'beautiful hypotheses are slain by ugly facts',[17] is both off-putting and seriously misleading. So here too there may be clues as to how school science could be improved so as to convey a picture of science that is at the same time both more accurate and more appealing.

Some of these concerns have already filtered through into curriculum prescriptions – though it remains to be seen how well they will prosper. The National Curriculum for science for England and Wales, for example, now contains an attainment target (AT number 17) on the 'nature of science', which requires science teachers to pay some attention to science as an activity with a human side and a chequered history. At 'level of attainment' 7 (which should normally be tackled towards the end of the 11–14 age span) students should 'be able to give an historical account of a change in accepted theory. . .for example. . .Galileo's dispute with the Church'. Yet the message that science develops as a matter of debate and social attribution, as well as of evidence and logic, is implicitly countermanded by sixteen other 'attainment targets', each of which is completely saturated with the view of science as an Unquestionable Body of Certain Knowledge.

It is not hard to see that the good intentions of AT17 are likely in practice to be dealt with by a didactic lesson, or a reading assignment, on Galileo and the Church, which will repeat the simplistic text-book analysis that Galileo was Brave and Clever, while The Church (whatever or whoever *that* was) was Powerful and Stupid. . .and then we can all heave a sigh of relief and get back to dissections and titrations. Unless the new message is made to permeate the old medium, the old medium is going to win out; and the new message will suffer the familiar Death by Tacking On. One can imagine forthcoming generations of students earnestly copying into their notebooks 'Science is a body of conjectures of the human imagination' – without them (or maybe even their teachers) having any sense of the irony of treating this statement as if it were itself another incontrovertible, eternal truth.

## SECONDARY SCIENCE

There is one other current trend that I ought to mention in order to complete this scene-setting. For much of the recent past science education has concerned itself with what goes on in secondary schools, and specifically with the tension between the needs of younger and less academic students on the one hand, and those of the older and quicker-to-grasp students on the other. The latter group, those who are relatively good at science and like it, pose a well-defined problem that is relatively well tackled: how to prepare them for vocational training and/or further study in science. Even if the demands of universities and employers cannot always be satisfied, nevertheless they are fairly clear, and meeting them largely involves extensions and amendments to the traditional activities of school science. For this group, which can be seen as somewhere in the middle of an educational journey, the problems concern how to prepare them for each stage, and how to design each so that it leads successfully to the next. The other group, the majority, will conclude their formal study of science at 16, and the task of education must therefore be seen as a preparation not for further supervised learning, but for life; and this is a much harder goal to define – as we have already seen. The dilemma in secondary school is how to meet both sets of needs, and whether it is possible to hit both targets with the same shot.

There is growing doubt as to whether it is – not least amongst secondary school science teachers themselves. The tension between the transmission of established ideas and the permission of individual exploration is especially strong in the early years of secondary school, and it is one which many science teachers find quite uncomfortable. In addition, they often experience a complementary problem: they know the regulation science only too well, enjoy its familiarity and its neat and tidy unfolding, and as a consequence feel apprehensive about straying off the beaten track into more controversial or less predictable areas. It is with the 11–14 age group, in my opinion, that this discomfort is felt by many teachers most acutely, and it is indeed where science education goes most badly wrong. Year after year teachers watch generations of students arrive with relatively open minds and high hopes at 11, knowing that by 14 many of them have decided that science is remote, hard and a dead loss. Yet they also feel at a loss to know what to do about it. It is on these teachers and the problems of this age group that much of the subsequent discussion will focus.

## PRIMARY SCIENCE

Though the debate about lower secondary science is the one that I shall concentrate on, concern has recently started to branch out in two other directions which must be borne in mind as important elements of the context of this debate. First there is the increasing emphasis on science education in the primary school. The younger the learners, the less plausible it is to base science lessons on watered-down or introductory versions of the textbook concepts that they might one day encounter – though this has been some people's approach. More common is the tendency to design, or ask the children to design, simple investigations into everyday phenomena (floating and sinking, rolling and throwing) or objects and animals. However the problems here tend to revolve around the teachers' grasp of a style of scientific activity that is more than 'nature study' but less than fully-fledged experimentation. In primary schools, science is the one area in which many teachers feel ill at ease, and there is a tendency for them to shy away from it. Their own experience of studying science at secondary school may well not have been a very happy one: many of them will have learnt to see 'science' as something that is too difficult to understand, and too technical to apply in real life. Seeing science as something that requires a lot of knowledge, expertise and (preferably) equipment, they feel both under-skilled and under-resourced. The new demands, both in Britain and elsewhere, mean that such teachers will no longer be able to avoid doing any 'science' at all, but if they are left with the implicit attitude that science proper is something much more hifalutin' than drawing leaves and looking after animals, their sense of intimidation may well remain – to colour their attitudes and to be transmitted to their students.

## HANDS–ON SCIENCE

The other direction in which science education is currently developing is the provision of out-of-school opportunities for firsthand exploration of interesting natural phenomena – the so-called 'hands on' movement, typified by the 'launch-pad' exhibition at the Science Museum in London, the 'exploratorium' in San Francisco, and mushrooming 'science parks' the world over. Bits of equipment are provided which allow a reasonable degree of unsupervised 'mucking about', and many of them are skilfully designed to produce a high degree of absorption and enthusiasm on the part of visitors (of all ages). These displays often generate something of the feel of involved exploration that many science teachers would give their eye teeth to have in their classrooms. The problem that they face, though, is that displays may derive at least part of their appeal precisely from the fact that they are unstructured, unassessed, and voluntary; and to the extent that this is so, any attempt to integrate them into a school-like curriculum, however ingenious the materials used, would be bound to fail. But if they are not incorporated into science education more formally, and school continues to be as unsatisfactory for some students as it is at present, it is hard to imagine that such exhibitions could ever have more than a marginal impact on young people's evolving attitudes and skills. Displays are caught in a kind of Catch 22: to have a significant effect they must 'work'; to 'work' they must be outside the mainstream educational system; but if they are outside the mainstream, they cannot have a significant effect.

## THE PLAN OF THE BOOK

Despite all the reflection and research of the last few years, science education is still in need of urgent improvement. Whatever the explanation – and the rest of this book is an attempt to *construct* a satisfactory explanation – the studies on science education, as well as a wealth of anecdote, reveal a situation that is not just mildly worrying but quite appalling. The research of recent years has produced some innovations and insights, but it has so far left a desperate situation substantially unchanged; and there is little reason to hope that any of the latest in a long line of innovations will of themselves bring about significant improvement in the enjoyment and mastery of science by the majority of students.

If after eight or more years of study a vast number of school-leavers cannot (or just as bad, will not) speak French, how much more serious is it that as many seem quite unable to engage with one of the most pivotal constituents of their *own* culture? Science education is giving cause for concern precisely because the disparity between its importance and its achievements is so wide. If it mattered less, its failures could be treated with greater equanimity. But because there are irrefutable reasons why some grasp of science is vital for the individual, for national economies, and for the well-being of the planet, the degree of disappointment that school science generates simply cannot be tolerated. Merely to devote more time to it, because it is so important, without ensuring that the time will be well spent, runs the risk of increasing the disappointment and frustration still further.

In order to remedy the situation science education needs to be – and is – conducting a number of urgent inquiries, and it is around these that the rest of this book is organised. Each of these represents an attempt to contrast the beliefs – sometimes explicit, sometimes tacit – on which science education has up till now been premised, with the best, most accurate alternatives which are currently available. In each case we need first to unearth what the actual working assumptions are, and to distinguish these from alternative beliefs which may form part of the rhetoric of the subject, but which are not really manifest in the way that science is taught in practice. And we then need to ask whether these implicit theories are accurate and appropriate. If we find that in some cases they are not, we need to undertake two further tasks: first – the easy bit – to identify a more solid foundation; and second, and much more difficult, to identify practicable strategies for getting this revised framework to take its place as the guiding mythology for teaching the subject in the minds of its teachers. It is on this last step that almost all educational reform is tripped up and rendered ineffective, and we shall have to return to it in some detail in the last chapter. For now, I wish to conclude this chapter with a rough outline of the areas of inquiry we shall visit, and some of the major lines of thought which will emerge.

The first step, after the overview provided by this chapter, must be to get an accurate participants' eye view of science education – first and foremost that of the students, but also that of the teachers. This is the business of Chapter 2. Despite the fact that some students find science fun, and learn to tackle it successfully, many, perhaps the majority, find it otherwise. They do not see its relevance to their life experiences and concerns; they do not realise its potential as an aid to dealing with the problems that they meet in their daily out-of-school lives; and they do not see it as internally coherent. At its worst, their experience is of a bitty, inconsequential, distant, difficult string of activities and episodes which demands much, and offers little in return.

Teachers for their part are often frustrated with the traditional procession of experimental demonstrations and canonical formulations of photosynthesis or acids and bases or the refraction of light. They too find it somewhat dull and lifeless, but feel stymied by the pressures of the curriculum, and the lack of any well-articulated alternative. Many also feel insecure when students ask smart questions that challenge the orthodox explanations, but for which the technical knowledge of their own degrees is either inappropriate, or inaccessible to the students. The only solution, unsatisfactory though it is, is to stick close to the safe formulae and forms of words, and try to give their students the basis for good results in exams.

Chapter 3 begins to dig below the surface of the current state of affairs by looking at the relationship between the experience of school science and the range and demands of problems that students meet in their out-of-school lives. The current rhetoric of science education stresses the usefulness of the skills that are developed in science lessons to the solution of problems encountered in everyday life. Yet there is no evidence that such transfer occurs, and good reasons to suppose that it will not. Some of these reasons relate to the arcane nature of scientific language and equipment; the demands in school to be explicit and logical in one's thought processes; the different social contexts and time pressures that typically apply; the criteria by which satisfactory solutions are recognised and judged; and above all intrinsic differences in the problem domains that are encountered.

In Chapter 4 I shall turn to a discussion of the image of science that is embedded in the practice of science education, and contrast this with some views that emerge as more accurate from a brief survey of approaches to the philosophy and sociology of science. People have attempted to define science as a 'noun' – i.e. as a body of knowledge – and as a 'verb' – as a particular method for the generation of knowledge. Both approaches have proved difficult to sustain. Both facts and theories turn out to be more difficult to pin down than school science makes them look: facts turn out to be permeated with human ideas, and theories form complicated tangles of ideas that often seem to have a life of their own. And the activities of science seem to depend very much on the nature, and especially on the stage of development, of the particular science you happen to be talking about. If there is such a thing as scientific thinking, it is at best a variable component of a much broader *modus operandi*, which includes styles of thought that are much less logical and explicit.

Another important question is: 'how are scientific claims evaluated, checked and established?' The school model of this is a completely rational one; scientists spot flaws in others' reasoning, and try to replicate their results. In fact a much more subtle, social process is at work, in which those with established reputations in a field make judgements about the *experimenter* which are at least as influential as those about the results. If we want students to 'understand something of the real world of science', just how much of its irrationality do we want them to know?

The final question is: 'what makes a scientist?' A scientist has mastered the activities, knowledge base, and 'style' of a given field, and may also possess certain qualities of tolerance for uncertainty; patience and persistence; independence and creativity. There is a dimension, in scientific work, that runs between 'routine science' and 'frontier science'. Whilst those students who want to study specialist science at school or university will need the skills, knowledge and attitudes of the routine scientist, I shall argue that *all* young people are in need of the abilities and attitudes that tend to be more characteristic of the frontier scientist. I shall emphasise especially the independence of mind needed to evaluate one's own and other people's ideas; and the particular mode of thought, which I shall call 'straight thinking', that leads from evidence about the way the world *is*, to well-educated guesses and predictions about the way it *might be*.

Chapter 5 turns to psychology, and contrasts the theories of learning that have been implicit in science education with a more contemporary approach. This rests on a number of general principles. The *constructive* principle says learning is not a passive registering of knowledge but an individual constructive process, drawing on pre-existing knowledge and learning strategies, and influenced by both situation-specific and long-term priorities. Science educators have recently been studying learners' pre-existing ideas about scientific topics, but, with the decline of Piaget's dominance, have rather neglected the role of learning styles and processes. Learners have 'theories' about everything; but their theories, unlike those of the professional scientist, are often very local and piecemeal. The principle of *modularity* says that the primary organisation of the young person's mind is into packages of knowledge and skill that are dedicated to particular familiar domains of experience. Science education has largely assumed that cognitive processes are content-free.

The *developmental* principle suggests that some broad trends are discernible over the course of a person's early life. Knowledge is gradually 'disembedded' from idiosyncratic details of the personal contexts in which it was first formulated, enabling it to be used more generally and powerfully. Language expands still further the internal flexibility of the child's knowledge. If children are in some sense scientists from the start, developing and testing their theories as they go along, their style as scientists nevertheless changes as they grow up. Only after a long process of evolution can they finally emerge as scientists in the intellectual sense. This evolution depends on the last principle, the *strategic* one, which says that certain important processes, as they grow in scope and strength, can come to function as 'cognitive tools' or 'learning strategies', and that the development of these can be amplified and fostered by specific forms of coaching and tuition. The aim of science education to develop these kinds of powers can only be successful if it is pursued with some understanding of what they are, and the conditions under which they evolve.

Recognition of these principles gives a better grasp on the perennial problem of the lack of transfer of skill and knowledge acquired under one set of conditions to other, even apparently quite similar, conditions. Science education is uniquely equipped to promote the disembedding of personal knowledge so that it becomes more widely available; the refining of informal modes of enquiry into more robust, logical and successful ones;

the discovery of the proper limits of 'scientific' forms of problem solving; and the development of the higher-order learning strategies that rely on self-awareness and reflectivity.

In Chapter 6 the insights of the preceding chapters are brought to bear on an analysis of the aims and priorities of science teaching. A range of possible aims is described, and their feasibility, compatibility and desirability are discussed in the light of the preceding reviews. These indicate that some traditional aims of science education – and particularly some combinations of aims – are unobtainable; while other opportunities and priorities are opened up. Science education in the 11–14 age range has the potential to consolidate vital *attitudes* to learning and the handling of uncertainty; and to promote the evolution and consolidation of important learning *abilities*, especially the habit of 'thinking straight' about practical and technological problems, and the intuitive appreciation of the benefits – and limitations – of deductive and inductive forms of inference.

These attitudes and abilities cannot be promoted, however, if the teacher is simultaneously trying to achieve the aim of transmitting a body of knowledge, or of producing some proficiency in accepted laboratory procedure. Recent talk of 'process skills' has obscured this incompatibility by confusing cognitive abilities with experimental competence. Being able to do a neat experiment does not guarantee that you understand what you did, or why you did it. By ignoring the limits of applicability of scientific thinking, and the difficulties involved in getting mental skills to function in contexts different from those in which they were learnt, science educators have recently produced a spate of grandiose rhetoric about the aims of science education that has badly confused teachers about what is possible and what is desirable.

Finally, in Chapter 7, we shall look at some suggestions for reform, and some of the problems associated with trying to promote reform in science education. One set of barriers is to be found in the legislation and prescriptions that curtail the freedom of teachers to experiment with their practice, but other continuing blocks to the necessary reforms are the attitudes, interests and anxieties of the existing generation of secondary school science teachers. For a variety of reasons, some good and many very understandable, many of them are unwilling to let go of the familiar and comfortable procedures and formulae of the science laboratory – even though they know, or sense, that a large proportion of students are benefiting little from their efforts.

In the light of this I shall propose some specific reforms. First, science at the 11–14 stage should focus exclusively on the development of lo-tech scientific attitudes and aptitudes that have genuine real-life utility. This stage should be protected from the demands of formal science. Teachers should be encouraged to choose whether to opt into or out of this new mode of teaching. Second, science at 14–16 should contain a substantial and on-going thread focusing on current controversies in the realm of science, both those of a theoretical nature (cosmology; organisation and function of the human brain) and those with direct social implications (nuclear power; global warming). Third, in-service training of a clearly identified kind must be provided for those teachers who would like to learn to let go of the content, and become 'coaches' of disciplined inquiry and straight thinking. And fourth, initial training of science teachers needs to be revised so that all new teachers are willing and able to focus, when appropriate, on science as a mode of thinking that may be completely divorced, in the early stages of its development, not only from the concepts and theories of received scientific wisdom, but also from the familiar procedures of the laboratory. This will in turn require a change of attitude and a re-skilling of those involved in training science teachers.[18]

NOTES

[1] From a talk by Margaret Thatcher to the Royal Society's Annual Dinner in 1988.

[2] These statistics were cited by Colin Blakemore in his presidential address 'Who cares about science?' to the British Association for the Advancement of Science Annual Meeting, Sheffield, September, 1989.

[3] Reported in *The Independent*, 20 June 1990.

[4] Assessment of Performance Unit, *Science at Age 15*, HMSO, London, 1988.

[5] See my chapter 'Cognition doesn't matter if you're scared, depressed or bored' in Philip Adey (ed.) *Adolescent Development and School Science*, Falmer: London, 1989.

[6] See *Science*, 3 Feb. 1988, p.600. This survey has since been replicated in modified form, with similar results, in a study by Glynis Breakwell, University of Surrey, which was reported in *The Sunday Times*, 22 April 1990.

[7] *The Guardian*, 14 May 1990.

[8] S. Sjoberg and S. Lie, 'Ideas about force and movement among Norwegian pupils and students', University of Oslo Institute of Physics Report **81–11**, 1981.

[9] M. McCloskey, 'Intuitive physics', *Scientific American*, **248**, 114–22, 1983.

[10] R.A. Griggs and S.E. Ransdell, 'Scientists and the selection task', *Social studies in science*, **16**, 319–30, 1987; S.L. Jackson and R.A. Griggs, 'Education and the selection task', *Bulletin of the Psychonomic Society*, **26**, 327–330, 1988; D.R. Lehman, R.O. Lempert and R.E. Nesbitt, 'The effects of graduate training on reasoning', *American Psychologist*, **43**, 431–442, 1988.

[11] D.N. Perkins, 'Post-primary education has little impact on informal reasoning', *Journal of Educational Psychology*, **77**, 562–71, 1985. For a general review of attempts to teach thinking directly, see R.S. Nickerson, D.N. Perkins and E.E. Smith, *The Teaching of Thinking*, Lawrence Erlbaum Associates: Hillsdale, NJ, 1985.

[12] A.A. Hyde and M.Bizar, *Thinking in Context: Teaching cognitive processes across the elementary school curriculum*, Longman: New York, 1989.

[13] For example, Rosalind Driver, *The Pupil as Scientist*, Open University Press: Milton Keynes, 1983.

[14] See P.J. Fensham, 'Science for all: a reflective essay', *Journal of Curriculum Studies*, **17**, 415–35, 1985.

[15] For example a recent survey by the Institute of Biology showed that teachers perceived a sharp drop in the standard of 'A' level biology, and no improvement in theoretical work, or in students' ability to study on their own, following the introduction of GCSE courses. As reported in *the Independent*, 28 July 1990.

[16] Driver, *op. cit.*; Richard White, *Learning Science*, Blackwell: Oxford, 1988; Roger Osborne and Peter Freyberg, *Learning in Science*, Heinemann: Auckland, 1985; Joseph Novak and Bob Gowin, *Learning How to Learn*, CUP: Cambridge, 1984.

[17] Quoted by W.I.B. Beveridge, *The Art of Scientific Investigations*, Mercury: London, 1961.

[18] Further reading for this chapter includes the following. Peter Fensham's edited collection *Development and Dilemmas in Science Education*, Falmer Press: London, 1988 gives a good overview of current issues. Jerry Wellington's collection *Skills and Processes in Science Education*, Routledge: London, 1989 takes a welcome critical look at the current fashion for emphasising so-called 'skills and processes', and down-playing the 'content'. Philip Adey's collection *Adolescent Development and School Science*, Falmer: London, 1989 gives a more psychological view. The influential books on learning science mentioned in the text are: Driver, *op. cit.*; Richard White, *Learning Science*, Blackwell: Oxford, 1988; Osborne and Freyberg, *op. cit.*; Joseph Novak and Bob Gowin, *Learning How to Learn*, CUP: Cambridge, 1984. Recent classics that relate more to the specifics of classroom practice are Michael Shayer and Philip Adey's *Towards a Science of Science Teaching*, Heinemann: London, 1981, and Brian Woolnough and Terry Allsop's *Practical Work in Science*, CUP: Cambridge, 1985.

———— · ————

# CHAPTER TWO

# ALICE THROUGH THE MICROSCOPE

The day I went into physics class it was death. A short dark man with a high lisping voice, named Mr. Manzi, stood in front of the class in a tight blue suit holding a little wooden ball. He put the ball on a steep grooved slide and let it run down to the bottom. Then he started talking about let *a* equal acceleration and let *t* equal time and suddenly he was scribbling letters and numbers and equals signs all over the blackboard and my mind went dead.

Sylvia Plath

Before I begin to explore some of the problems that both students and teachers experience with school science, let me reiterate that there are many exceptions to the general picture that I am going to paint: many, but not enough. There are students who derive pleasure and benefit from their science, and not all of them are 'bright' ones, destined for post-compulsory study and university degrees. Some have a cast of mind that makes science intelligible and interesting. And others are capable of becoming intrigued, and of enjoying grappling with scientific problems and concepts, some of the time, depending on the intrinsic nature of the topic, their own changing interests, and the skill and energy of the teacher. Of course there are good teachers, just as there are enthusiastic students: I heard only the other day of a science teacher in Canberra, Australia who, having been on an in-service course in science teaching that changed her whole approach to the subject, was now embarrassed to find herself pursued down the corridor after lessons by two dozen fourteen-year-olds chanting 'We want more science; we want more science.'

And some teachers inspire not only enthusiasm but also a high degree of achievement. W.J. Fletcher wrote in the *New Zealand Science Teacher* in 1979:

There is one great mystery behind science teaching that Jerome Bruner has called our attention to. Why is it that some teachers consistently produce fine science students? I don't mean just good examination passers, but people who are fired up with interest in science, and who go on to produce fine research. Some secondary teachers do this. Some university professors are famous for it.

Something goes on in the classes of these outstanding people that makes a
difference to the pupils. There is, as Bruner says, some kind of method, some
kind of enthusiasm, that is being conveyed. And it obviously has something to
do with confidence and imagination.[1]

Sadly this is a mystery only in the context of what is widely agreed to
be 'normal': a far more prevalent lack of both commitment and comprehension on the part of a great many young people. This contrasting
state of affairs is familiar to almost every secondary science teacher, and has
been documented again and again in surveys and observations of students'
attitudes and behaviour. My review, though therefore not for the most
part original, is necessary as a springboard for the analysis that follows. I
intend it to be uncompromising, but not damning; a foundation of realism
on which to build a critique and a way forward.

## EXPECTATIONS OF SCIENCE

Young people's reactions to science lessons are a function not only of what
happens in the lessons, but also of what they hoped or expected would
happen. Disappointment is, here as always, a product of expectation. So
in what frame of mind might 11-year-olds, let us say, approach the subject
of science? It will depend in large part on their experiences at primary
school. They might have had a lot of what was called 'science' and enjoyed
it. They might have done exactly the same things but without thinking of
them as 'science'. Many of them will have been familiar with some of the
language of science – they may have acquired a basic or not-so-basic idea
of what an 'experiment' or a 'fair test' is, for example. In England and
Wales, as the provisions of the National Curriculum begin to work their
way into practice, all entrants to secondary science will be quite conversant
with ways of measuring, examining and talking about a range of phenomena within their day-to-day experience. They will probably have
carried out investigations on plants, soil, small animals and waste and refuse.
They will have been given a very rough idea of how bodies work, and told
about the dangers of drugs, household chemicals, and hot chip-pans. They
will have been introduced to electricity and simple circuits, and explored
the behaviour of magnets and computers. They will have found some
things out about sounds and colours.

The majority will have enjoyed their investigations of a variety of things,
seeing how they behave, and they will have begun to get a sense of what
experiments are for, and how they are designed. They will have an image
of science as an activity that *observes* and *records* natural phenomena, and
*asks questions* about how they came to be the way they are, and why they
work the way they do. They will not yet have a sense, most of them, of

the relationship between science and technology on a grander scale; of the formality and complexity of scientific explanations; of the social issues concerning science and its products; or of the potential of scientific thinking as a learning tool in their own lives.

Whatever their school experience, however, they are bound to have picked up images about what science is, and what kinds of people scientists are, from their out-of-school lives. Casual acquaintance with stereotypes such as that expressed by Ogden Nash may well have left their mark:[2]

I give you now Professor Twist,
A most pedantic scientist.
Trustees exclaimed 'He never bungles'
And sent him off to distant jungles.
Camped by a tropic riverside,
One day he missed his loving bride;
She had, the guide informed him later,
Been eaten by an alligator.
Professor Twist could not but smile:
'You mean', he said, 'a crocodile.'[3]

Certainly they will have seen mad scientists and scatter-brained professors on the television – David Bellamy, Magnus Pike, Patrick Moore and co. will have shown them that 'scientists' are often zany – along with serious-looking men (and less frequently women) in white coats whose pronouncements are treated as more weighty than ordinary people's. They will know that washing machines are supposed to be better if they are sold as 'The Appliance of Science', and washing powders are better if they are 'biological'. *Tomorrow's World* or *Ripley's Believe it or not!* may have taught them that science is to do with machines and chemicals and the discovery of things that are faster or cleaner or which make life easier.

More serious programmes on radio and TV, together with conversations they have overheard or taken part in, may have introduced them to concepts like 'evolution' or 'black holes': *Horizon* and the odd Open University programme, watched out of boredom on a wet Sunday morning, may have introduced the idea that science is also about weighing up competing explanations, and can be controversial, while at the other extreme there are *Star Wars*, *Batman* and *Teenage Mutant Ninja Turtles* to confuse them thoroughly about what is actual, what is possible, and what is unrealisable fantasy. 'You'll believe a man can fly,' said the posters for the first *Superman* movie, and there will have been many young members of the audience who did.

Different young people will arrive with different stews of half-false, half-understood, half-conscious ideas about what science is and what it has discovered. Most of them, unless they have older brothers and sisters to put them straight, will be expecting 'science' to be informative, surprising and fun. What in fact do they find? What are some of the more common ingredients of the science students' disillusionment?

## Bittiness

The first ingredient of many students' experience of science is its fragmentary nature. Despite the fact that teachers feel that lessons within a block of work form a well-planned and logical progression, this overview and sense of coherence and cumulativeness is often quite absent from the students' perception. Lessons are seen as isolated events, self-contained, and either interesting and comprehensible in their own right or not, but bearing little relation to what has gone before. For example, a teacher who was involved in a lesson that required students to observe the effect of heat on the dissolving of potassium permanganate crystals told an observer:

> This is a third lesson in a series aimed at developing a particle idea and going over states of matter. . .the first one we did was also to do with this. It was to do with expansion and contraction of substances – today was a direct follow-on from that.[4]

One might question the coherence of this teacher's rationale, but she very clearly had some overall picture of what the block of work was about. Typical of the students' perception of the lesson, however, was this comment:

> Observer: 'What was today's lesson about?'
> Robert: 'What crystals can do.'
> Observer: 'Does today's work have anything to do with this other work you have been doing?' (pointing to the student's open exercise book which was showing notes with headings such as 'the dilution of a potassium permanganate crystal' and 'heating and expanding liquids').
> Robert: 'No, not really. . .no.'

Even when some sense of the 'story-line' of a series of lessons does begin to emerge, at least for some students, there may be a shift to a different block of work that nips this sense in the bud – and after a few such experiences, students may learn that there is little point in trying to keep up. One said:

> You just start to get to know what you're talking about and they [the teachers] change it [the topic]. . .you forget everything that you know. . .in the end you do not know what you are doing.

This development of what the psychologists call 'learned helplessness' is common in schools and very pernicious, for it leads students to protect themselves from the repeated experience of feeling foolish and looking ignorant by *not trying*.[5] Being perpetually at sea is an uncomfortable state, and it is made worse when you feel that no amount of exertion on your part is going to make any significant difference. Under such circumstances the major priority shifts from learning to self-preservation, and this may take a number of forms, from adopting a kind of shell of tactical stupidity, to becoming invisible, to mucking about or even truanting.[6] Many teachers are familiar with the class that collectively averts its eyes and sinks into sullen silence as they, the teachers, with mounting frustration and bewilderment, ask a series of increasingly trivial questions. 'I can't believe they are that thick,' they might bemoan to a colleague after the lesson – and they are right not to. At such times the 'game' is not achievement but the defence of a threatened self-esteem.

Learned helplessness is also a disastrous state to produce in students because it is so hard to reverse. One they have stopped looking for meaning in what is happening, they will not see it, even if it reappears. Thus a clumsy or inarticulate teacher may cause students to disengage from their subject in a way that is effectively irreversible. It is not just that they switch off; they take out the fuse and throw it away.[7]

## Invisible Structure

Although secondary school science often feels like a collection of isolated experiences, nevertheless students know that there is some supposed order, some string on which the individual beads of their experience could be strung. Even though they do not see what it is, there is clearly a sequence which has to be followed, and which does not allow for side-turnings or serendipity. A British science educator asked her teenage daughter to describe the difference, as she experienced it, between the science she did at primary school and what she was now doing at secondary. She said primary science was like being in a small plane flying over a vast open landscape like a desert. You could land anywhere to have a look around and explore for a while. There was a sense in which it didn't seem to matter too much *where* you had landed, because it was the exploring that was important, not so much what you found. The fact that the knowledge you accumulated was patchwork, and had big 'holes' in it was not a problem.

Secondary science, on the other hand, was like being on a train in carriages that had blanked-out windows. You were going in a single direction, about which you had no choice. The train stopped at every station and you had to get off, whether you liked it or were interested or not, and pay attention to what the train driver told you to. Then you got back on the train and went off to the next station – but because the windows were opaque you could not see the countryside in-between, so you did not know how the stations were linked or related to each other. Obviously you were on a purposeful journey, you were going somewhere,

*[handwritten margin note: Analogy]*

and the train driver seemed to know where it was. Worst of all was the feeling that you were supposed to understand the direction of the journey too, even though nobody had given you a map, or let you look out of the train as it was chugging along. So there was a risk that you would come to think that it was your fault that you could not put it all together.

## Pointlessness

Given this lack of a framework to give purpose or direction to activities in the science laboratory, it is not surprising that students frequently do not *see* the point of exercises or experiments, even if they have, in the teacher's terms, been well explained. If students are not to give up and drift aimlessly, which many of them do, they cling to what fragments of sense they can: they try to follow instructions to the letter, or to achieve what they imagine to be the desired result by whatever means they can. Two students were observed heating a yellow solid; their commentary went like this:

> Observer: 'What are you doing now?'
> Keith: 'Heating this.'
> O: 'I see, what for?'
> K: 'Well. . .(races off to desk on other side of the room; brings back book)...we are doing No.5.'
> O: 'What did you do before you started heating it?'
> K: 'These ones here.' (indicating Nos 3 and 4 of the instructions).
> O: 'Can you tell me what you have found out?'
> K: 'We got this yellow stuff.'
> O: 'Can you tell me the purpose of this activity?'
> K: 'No. . .not really.'

As the observer in this little scene notes, science teachers may find themselves in something of a Catch 22 situation with respect to experimental instructions, if they are dealing with students who lack, as Keith does, any feel for the purpose or context of what they are doing. If you do not give them clear, explicit, detailed instructions, they are likely to flounder, having no scientific common sense to fall back on. But if you *do* provide such instructions, giving students a fail-safe recipe for carrying out the experiment, you are in danger of reinforcing precisely the low level of intellectual involvement that gave rise to the problem in the first place. You are encouraging students to become even more mechanical and uncomprehending in their attitude to science.

## Falsification

Even worse than this, students may be reduced to fabricating results and simulating understanding in their increasingly desperate attempt to find some satisfaction and meaning in what they are being asked to do. We are not talking here about the odd student who 'cheats' in order to gain an advantage in a test. We are talking about an epidemic of falsification, in which teachers very often, whether they are aware of it or not, collude. In a general science lesson a little while ago I witnessed a not-uncommon kind of occurrence. The class were doing the standard test to see whether plant matter produced carbon dioxide under a variety of conditions, using the indicator bromothymol blue. The class had been told that the indicator was supposed to turn yellow in the presence of $CO_2$. A 12-year-old girl sitting in front of me had produced a sample with a rather nice turquoise colour, and looking for reassurance, and anxious not to make a mistake, she showed it to the teacher and asked if she could write down that the indicator had turned 'bluey-green'. 'What did I tell you happened?' asked the teacher. 'It goes yellow,' remembered the girl. 'Well then, that's what you write down,'was the reply. A little later the same teacher, cheerfully explaining to the class that a sample she had prepared had not 'worked properly', concocted something that looked the 'right' colour, and talking to me over the heads of the group said, 'I cheat a lot, don't I girls?'

A student of mine a few years ago asked a class of 14-year-olds to write down the meanings of some common scientific terms. In response to the word 'conclusion', several of them had written: 'That's where we write down what *should* have happened.'

Here is another exchange from the book by Osborne and Freyberg. Two 14-year-old girls have failed to see any change in an experiment and have just asked the teacher 'what should have happened'.

> Stephanie: 'Oh, it is not going to work, Aileen. . .we will just pretend it changed.'
> Aileen: 'Yes.'
> Observer: 'Is that what you do when it doesn't work. . .pretend it worked. . . .So what do you write down? What do you think should have happened?'
> S: 'Yes. . .we found out nothing.'
> A: 'Oh, it is not going to happen. . .too bad.'
> O: 'What happens if you write down what actually happens?'
> A: (Giggle, shrug.)
> O: 'Why do you feel you have to write down what should have happened rather than what actually happened?'
> A: 'Because it would be a waste of time. . .we would be doing it for nothing.'
> O: 'I see. If you wrote down what you got rather than what you should have got?'
> A: 'Yeah. . .so now we know we are failures.'
> O: 'And nobody else is going to know if you write down what you should have got; is that right?'
> S: 'Yes.'
> A: 'If we write down what we should have got then she'd [the teacher] think it's what we would have got, then we get more points!'
> O: 'Oh well, I wonder if anyone else got it [the expected result]; or do they all

do what you do?'
Both students smile!

By going along with this wide-spread practice (whether knowingly or in blissful ignorance) teachers are developing a number of attitudes that they might on reflection rather not. First they are encouraging a cynical and casual attitude towards observation. Why should you bother to observe with detail and precision when what you see turns out so often to be 'wrong'? Secondly they are fostering an instrumental rather than an inquisitive attitude towards science, and perhaps towards school work more generally. The job is to please the teacher and get good marks; not to exercise one's mental muscles as hard as one can. Thirdly the medium is reinforcing the message – regardless of what the teachers themselves actually say – that science education is about remembering the results of other people's research ('facts') rather than developing the ability to conduct one's own. As I shall argue, there is nothing wrong at all with adopting this as an explicit goal of science teaching. It is a perfectly valid aim to want young people to know something of the content of 'official' science. The problems arise when you pretend you are doing something else, like helping them to sharpen their powers of observation. . .*then* they start to get confused.

### Illogicality

Although one of the cornerstones of the so-called 'scientific method' is a scrupulous concern with the quality of inferences, school science some-times asks students to accept quite illogical deductions. They might be invited to drop a piece of magnesium strip into a test-tube containing dilute hydrochloric acid, and to verify that the gas produced, if collected in another test-tube, ignites with the time-honoured squeaky pop. If all goes according to plan – by no means a foregone conclusion even in this simple experiment – students are then invited to 'conclude' from this experience that 'metals react with acids to produce hydrogen'. This is neither a rational deduction, nor a true one, yet it is a rare student and a rare teacher who will have a profitable exchange about its dubious nature. It is, to use another example with whiskers on it, as if students had been shown a white swan, and then invited to conclude that this 'proved' that all swans were white.

Another instance comes from work by Sara Delamont,[8] in which she records a student's reaction to the very common classroom experiment designed to show that starch forms only in those parts of a leaf that are directly exposed to sunlight, and not in areas that have been covered with spots of aluminium foil. Having done the requisite tests (which in this case seem to have revealed the desired results), the student is still unwilling to accept the suggested conclusion:

I don't see how that will prove it – it could be all sorts of things we don't know anything about. . .Well, you [addressing her teacher] said if there was starch in the bare patches it would mean that there was. . .it was because of the light, but it could be the chemicals in the foil, or something we know nothing about.

Here is a student being a much better – more cautious, more rational – scientist than her teacher; but if she wishes to pass her exams, she will be advised to swallow her qualms and remember the 'right answer'.

The problem again is not with the experiments as such, but with the way they are framed. They are actually demonstrations of useful (though limited) approximations to 'the truth', and seen in this light are defensible exercises. It is useful to see with your own eyes an illustration of a more general principle that you are actually being asked to accept on the authority of the teacher. But as soon as there is any suggestion that students are at the same time 'doing science', in the sense of discovering valid generalisations on the basis of their own observations, two entirely different kind of operation are being horribly confused, and the brighter ones at least will start to get uncomfortable, though most will not have a clear enough grasp of the situation to know why. It may be just these students, the ones who, perhaps unwittingly, are too intelligent to accept the half-truths that they are being proffered, who escape from the discomfort by dropping science; and it may therefore not be too fanciful to suggest that science education in the lower secondary school serves to select a second-class or compliant pool of candidates for specialist study and university science.

Demonstration and investigation are not the only kinds of practical activity that students are asked to undertake. As they get older, for example, they will find themselves doing 'practicals' more and more in order to develop and practice certain laboratory skills. Here again is a perfectly useful bit of 'prevocational training' – some students will need to be able to get 'good results' in their titrations or distillations as they proceed to work or further study. And all students, it could be argued, need to be able to weigh and measure with care if science's interesting observations are to appear to them. But in such a practical, there is clearly a known and correct value or product to be found, and students' success is properly gauged by how close their results come to this standard. Here again, if they are also led to believe that they are behaving like 'real scientists', rather than like apprentices, the main result is likely to be not distillation but stupefaction.

There is another more subtle but equally important reason why it is not permissible to expect students to be able to replicate the experiments of science proper – carrying out simplified versions of classical procedures, and making essentially the same observations as those of the original experimenters. Even if they replicated the experiment exactly, they would not see the same things, because they are looking through eyes that are differently tuned. As we shall see in more detail in Chapter 4, scientific observations are heavily imbued with the beliefs of the observer. So 'to claim, for example, that when a child looks down a spinthariscope he is seeing what Rutherford saw, and stands in the same relation to the experimental evidence as Rutherford did, is to assume that perception is unaffected by previous experience, knowledge, and expectations. This is clearly not so.'[9]

## Carelessness

In science lessons students are for ever being told to do things 'carefully'. This often seems to have little effect on their experimental precision: as we saw in Chapter 1, a recent national survey in Britain showed just how astonishingly clumsy and imprecise they are.[10] It is not only that people have been telling them to 'be careful' since they were babies, an injunction that they probably associate as much with being deprived of fun as with a concern for personal safety. It is because, lacking a *feel* for science, they do not have an intuitive appreciation of the value of accuracy, and therefore construe it as a demand imposed on them by the authority of the teacher, rather than as something that arises naturally from the nature of science. Thus operations are performed sloppily; thus results are aberrant and uninteresting; thus the students feel failures; and thus science lessons become even less meaningful, and still more distasteful.

Several of the points I have made so far are summarised in an article by Janet Daley published in *The Independent* on 22 November 1989. She speaks from the point of view of a parent rather than of a teacher or a researcher, but her points echo strongly those substantiated more formally. She asks:

> Why should so many people be put off the study of science at school? I have talked to a number of children. . .from a number of schools, both state and private. What emerged was a sense of the mind-deadening boredom of school science. Only the occasional inspired teacher managed to transcend the tedium of the syllabus and its prescribed treatment.
>
> From what the children said, the sciences were treated as closed-ended collections of facts to be memorised without discussion or insight. This conception of science as an accumulation of fixed data was conveyed through an endless series of experiments which were carried out in a thoroughly unexperimental way, which is to say, with results which were foregone conclusions. The notion of true experimentation and its relation to hypothesis was almost entirely neglected. . .[It is] a profoundly anti-intellectual approach in which scientific-*like* activity is substituted for understanding of scientific concepts. Ironically the activity itself is often spurious. My daughter has commented that in the imperfect conditions of the school laboratory, the experiments frequently do not 'work' and must then be falsified in the writing-up to show the required result. In all these show-and-tell exercises, there seems to be little reference to

any broad understanding of science as an arena for debate and originality. . .The simplemindedness of much of the experimentation, which serves only to demonstrate the most basic of principles, struck many of the children as time-wasting. . .It is the apparent pointlessness of much activity-based science which alienates so many of the brightest children.

## Difficulty

For many students science very quickly becomes hard work mentally: it requires a lot of brain-strain. In the place of the looked-for uncertainty and thrill of finding out, they begin to find exercises that centre on mathematics and equations of various sorts. So unless they are also passably good at sums, they may find that physical science especially begins to stretch them beyond their limits. Concepts begin to be introduced that are remote from their everyday experience, and which therefore cannot be grasped in terms of that experience; yet these concepts often seem to be pivotal to students' future understanding of, and thus success in, the subject. The concepts of the 'mole' in chemistry, 'respiration' in biology or 'capacitance' in physics are internal to the subject: they derive their meaning from a whole framework of theory that the subject presupposes, yet which may be quite obscure to the students at the time the concepts are introduced.

Consider the concept of 'energy', for example, which is central not just to one but to all three of the main school science subjects. Biologists tend to talk of energy in terms of an energy flow from the sun down through the world of living things. Physicists use the term energy in the sense of 'work being done', and as a quantifiable variable in equations, while chemists talk of energy in the context of the behaviour of chemicals and the conditions and direction of their reactions. Yet the three different frameworks and usages are very rarely brought into conjunction, and their overlaps and contradictions, in so far as they are sensed by students at all, have to be dealt with in a private way that contains, but does not resolve, the confusion. Many science teachers themselves are unable to do much better. And on top of this students bring to science lessons a vast array of personal meanings and connotations for the word 'energy': 'energy is a fuel; it gets burnt and used up, and we ought to conserve it'; 'food gives me energy which I use up as I run around'; 'energy is a kind of force that gets things done'; 'nuclear energy is dangerous'; and so on.[11]

Thus students are sometimes being asked to learn definitions, ideas or operations, and to develop some fluency in their use, which can be tied neither to the world of common sense, nor to a clear, coherent theoretical infrastructure of the scientific topic. This may or may not be a necessary thing to demand of students: there *may* be ideas that have to be embedded with a pile-driver *before* they can be properly understood. But it is a hard thing to ask students to do because, as we shall see in Chapter 5, it requires a set of learning skills and attitudes that are more sophisticated than many 13-year-olds possess.

## Boredom

Young people often accuse school science of being boring, and it is worth considering the multitude, or at least the range, of sins that this most familiar of pejorative terms is used to cover. One thing it refers to is the lack of intrinsic excitement. Occasionally, and mostly early on in their secondary school careers, students are delighted by the 'stinks and bangs' they are allowed to experience. Most people can remember from their school science days the lesson in which they produced something they were actually allowed to *drink*; the time the tin filled with gas blew up; the day all the locusts got out; the sight of burly Mr Mandrake trying to get a hard-boiled egg into (and then out of) a milk bottle – and then casually making a sandwich with it as he told us about the expansion and contraction of gases; the time Dianne dropped the sodium into the sink. Whether planned or not, such experiences *are* exciting, and unless a more intellectual form of satisfaction begins to take over, as it does for some but not all students, then the predominant *lack* of attention-grabbing, intriguing experiences remains a lingering source of disappointment.

Second, science is often not illuminating. It neither deals with phenomena that students find personally important or problematic; nor does it offer theories and insights that seem helpful or – dreadfully overused word – relevant. Some typical student comments are:

> If we had done things in class that related to what happened everyday, that would have made it a lot more interesting.

> They relate it to things that you wouldn't think of, that don't really come into your life.

And teachers are only too aware of the same lack of appeal. They say things like:

> We are expecting that they will be interested in everything that we do . . .However quite a lot of what we do doesn't relate very directly to outside experiences.

> We just carry out the experiments that have been set down in the books. . .and they often don't really relate to the outside world.

One science educator, Peter Hewson, has proposed that people in general are disposed to accept a new theory only if it is perceived as *apposite* to a problem that they are currently trying to solve; *intelligible* in terms of their pre-existing ideas; *plausible*, in the sense of fitting with their beliefs, opinions and attitudes; and potentially *fruitful* in offering solutions to their problem.[12] For most science students, most of the time, these conditions are very far from being met, and there is a consequent reluctance to engage with them at any more than a superficial level.

## Impersonality

One central aspect of this lack of 'grip' is the increasingly impersonal nature of much of science. Neither physics-y nor chemistry-y types of science appeal to young people's overwhelming interest in *human* affairs, and this may explain the relative popularity of biological topics, especially with younger students and with girls. As one girl put it:

> I can relate to Biology more. . .to things around really. . .I mean I couldn't relate to things like in Physics. . .how we push something and it hits something off the end [of the bench, presumably]. . .well O.K., so it does it; so what?

Unless a subject has come to incorporate its own internal generator of curiosity and challenge, it has to depend for motivation on its relationship to pre-existing and continuing concerns that learners bring into the laboratory with them – concerns that from birth have revolved predominantly around the social worlds of people and, to an extent, of other animals. They can 'identify' with animals, and if necessary make them interesting by anthropomorphizing them. Even the sex life of the earthworm can be made lively if you use your imagination. . .even the behaviour of woodlice in a choice-chamber. But to get a class of 12-year-olds absorbed in the 'problem' of why a ball thrown in the air turns round and comes down again, or how come some white stuff turns yellow when you heat it, you usually have to work quite a lot harder.

Not only are young people interested in the animate world; they are used, from an early age, to overhearing, and then joining in, conversations about that world. Informal language is peppered with observations and comments on the behaviour of friends, relatives, people in the street, pet rabbits, animals at the zoo. They have learnt that it is normal and natural to speculate about the needs and habits of things that move under their own steam. The idea that the worlds of powders and coloured liquids, of pulleys, slopes and blocks, or of batteries and switches, could be just as much a source of fascination and inquiry, is one that does not come as readily to many young people. These domains are not *problematic* in anything like the same way, and their out-of-school life is much less likely to have accustomed them to talking as if they were (unless their parents are scientists or science teachers). Everyday life for the adolescent tends to follow the old American dictum, 'if it ain't broke, don't fix it', and while the social world is constantly on the edge of coming apart, the world of 'stuff' is much less fragile to the teenager. (We shall have more to say about this question of what needs explaining in the next chapter.)

The language of school science is designed to increase this impersonal feeling.[13] Students are mostly still taught that there is a form of words that they should use to report their investigations which conceals, as much as possible, the fact that *they* did them. 'A white solid was heated.' 'When the leaves were unwrapped they had turned brown.' It is as if science did itself, without the aid of fallible and often perplexed human operators who had needs, ideas and questions about what was going on. The world is purged of the social and physical context: how we were feeling, what the weather was like, how hot the lab was, what Lesley said to me while we were doing the experiment. . .all these things are washed away in the write-up, and the only traces of our activity left are Aim, Method, Results and Conclusion. The written world of school science, like that of the scientific paper which it is designed to ape, is not a world in which people marvel, guess, chat, change their minds, burn themselves, and forget vital stages of the procedure.[14]

## Evasion

When students are finding science hard to understand, they often find that their teachers are less help than they had hoped. What to the students seems a perfectly sensible question, born of a wish to figure out what something means, may be met with a reaction that does not mesh with their half-baked, but well-intentioned, ideas at all. Instead they are merely given a repetition of a formula, or a particular form of words, which, in the end, they simply have to commit to memory. It seems as if teachers are often reluctant, or perhaps afraid, to stray from the straight and narrow of definitions and worked examples, into areas where their own grasp of the concepts might become suspect.

Part of the problem that lies behind this apparent dogmatism is that most science teachers have not been equipped by their undergraduate degrees to deal with the questions of 11-year-olds. Their expert knowledge is too technical to be accessible to scientific novices, yet at the same time may be built on theoretical foundations that, despite the intricacy of the super-structure, are themselves rather shaky. Core concepts – like 'energy', as we have seen – may be well-embedded in the way they think, yet they may have a hard time of it to *explain* and *justify* them explicitly. When required to go back to first principles, and deprived of their maths and their machines, teachers who were quite competent undergraduate scientists may suddenly feel rather insecure, and be forced to fall back on the rigid definitions that the textbooks provide. Thus at crucial moments the rhetoric of inquiry is suddenly replaced with dogmatism and appeals to authority, and students may thereby discover that, after all, science is about remembering, not understanding.

Rae Munro, a New Zealand science educator, recently wrote:

About a year ago I became intrigued by the question of whether or not teachers did fully understand the big ideas that they taught. . .In all cases they admitted the topics were complex and that they didn't fully understand them. But at the same time, they all confided that they taught them *as if they had complete understanding.*

Their replies confirmed what I have long suspected is a major problem in science teaching and testing, namely, that we frequently *pretend* to greater knowledge and understanding than we actually possess and that, further, because we structure exam questions around much of our pretended knowledge we invite pupils to become 'successful' simply by modelling our own pretence.[15]

Osborne and Freyberg agree. 'Where the teacher's own concepts are inadequate', they say, 'there is unfortunately a greater likelihood that he or she will consciously or subconsciously try to obscure his or her lack of understanding by the use of technical language, whether it be verbalised, written on the board, or referenced from the textbook.'[16]

I do not mean or wish to imply that science teachers are particularly prone to retreat into rigidity, obscurity or authority when they feel insecure; only to point out that they are no different from the rest of us. There will be times when, as Douglas Barnes put it, 'the teacher, frightened by his sudden glimpse of the gulf between them' – i.e. him/herself and the students – 'hastily continues with the lesson he had planned'.[17] Not only do science teachers sometimes lack a store of ways of enriching a difficult topic, and making it accessible to young learners; they also, when put on the spot, do not model the spirit of inquiry terribly well. Instead of saying 'That's a really good question, and I don't know the answer. How are we going to find out?', they may in the heat of the moment, under the pressure of an overstuffed syllabus, turn to the blackboard and run through the catechism on photosynthesis or the atomic nucleus one more time.

Towards the end of the book I shall have to come back to the subject of the knowledge and attitudes of science teachers, because it is they, and not yet more bright ideas about how to teach science, that hold the key to its improvement. If they do not see a clear alternative to the present muddle of motives, are not given sufficient practical instruction in what this alternative means and requires, and do not understand what it will take to bring it into being, then there is no hope of its spirit, however enlightened, percolating into the day-to-day practices of school science labs around the country.

At the start of this chapter we met Sylvia Plath suffering brain death at the hands of a Mr. Manzi. By the time she had moved on to Mr. Manzi's chemistry class the following year, she had learnt how to cope with his enforced world of stupefying remoteness – and she reminds us that students have many ways to protect themselves from the effects that they might otherwise have suffered.

> I went to the chemistry class five times a week and didn't miss a single one. Mr. Manzi stood at the bottom of the big, rickety old amphitheatre, making blue flames and red flares and clouds of yellow stuff by pouring the contents of one test tube into another, and I shut his voice out of my ears by pretending it was only a mosquito in the distance and sat back enjoying the bright lights and the coloured fires and wrote page after page of villanelles and sonnets.[18]

## NOTES

[1] W.J. Fletcher, 'Science teaching: are we nurturing scientists or conformists?' *New Zealand Science Teacher*, **21**, 46–54, 1979.

[2] The British survey into children's scientific knowledge and attitudes commissioned by the Economic and Social Research Council, conducted by Dr Glynis Breakwell of the University of Surrey, found widespread agreement with the stereotype of scientists as intelligent but boring people who use long words (as reported in *The Sunday Times*, 22 April 1990).

[3] Ogden Nash, *Collected verse from 1929 on*, Dent: London, 1966.

[4] This and the other quotations from science lessons in this chapter are taken from Chapter 6 of Roger Osborne and Peter Freyberg, *Learning in Science*, Heinemann: Auckland, 1985, unless otherwise indicated.

[5] See for example, Carol Dweck, 'Motivational processes affecting learning', *American Psychologist*, **41**, 1040–8, 1986; Carol Dweck and Ellen Leggett, 'A social-cognitive approach to motivation and personality', *Psychological Review*, **95**, 256–73, 1988.

[6] For a review of defensive strategies, see my *Teaching to Learn: A direction for education*, Chapter 7, Cassell: London, 1990.

[7] The classic reference on 'learned helplessness' is Martin Seligman, *Learned Helplessness: On depression, development and death*, Freeman: San Francisco, 1975.

[8] See Michael Stubbs and Sara Delamont (eds), *Explorations in Classroom Observation*, Wiley: London, 1976. I am grateful to Miles Barker for drawing my attention to one of his favourite examples of school science penalising students for being good scientists.

[9] David Layton, *Science for the People*, Allen and Unwin: London, 1973.

[10] Assessment of Performance Unit, *Science at Age 15*, HMSO: London, 1988.

[11] These findings come from the Learning in Science Project (Energy), conducted at the Centre for Science and Mathematics Education Research at the University of Waikato, 1985–88. They are summarised in *Energy for a Change*, University of Waikato, New Zealand, 1989.

[12] Peter Hewson, 'A conceptual change approach to learning science', *European Journal of Science Education*, **3**, 383–96, 1981.

[13] See for example, Clive Sutton, 'Writing and reading in science: the hidden messages', in Robin Millar (ed.), *Doing Science: Images of science in science education*, Falmer: London, 1989.

[14] Even this rational residue is something of an intellectual fraud, in that it presents as a tidy sequence a collection of thought processes and operations that are inherently fuzzy and interwoven (see Chapter 4). This is well discussed by Sir Peter Medawar in a classic article called 'Is the scientific paper a fraud?', which is summarised in his excellent little book *Advice to a Young Scientist*, Pan: London, 1979.

[15] Rae Munro, 'The misrepresentation of science: a teacher's dilemma', *New Zealand Science Teacher*, **59**, 8–17, 1988–9.

[16] Osborne and Freyberg, *op. cit.*

[17] D. Barnes, *Language, the Learner and the School*, Penguin: London, 1969.

[18] For further reading on students' experience of science education, see Osborne and Freyberg, *op. cit.*; and also *Children's Ideas in Science*, edited by Rosalind Driver, Edith Guesne and Andree Tiberghien, Open University Press: Milton Keynes, 1985. For more on the experience of science in primary schools, see Wynne Harlen, *Teaching and Learning Primary Science*, Harper and Row: London, 1985. The way in which 'practicals' confuse students is described by Brian Woolnough and Terry Allsop, *Practical Work in Science*, CUP: Cambridge, 1985. Students' emotional and defensive reactions in lessons are discussed in my *Teaching to Learn*, *op.cit.* The way in which young people pick up scientific ideas from the media is analysed by Neil Ryder in his *Science, Television and the Adolescent*, Independent Broadcasting Authority: London, 1979.

# CHAPTER THREE

———  ·  ———

# LAB-LAND AND THE REAL WORLD

Had it been only stories that didn't measure up to the world it wouldn't have been so bad. But it wasn't only fiction that was fiction. Fact too was fiction, as text books seemed to bear no more relation to the real world than did the story books. At school or in my *Boy's Book of the Universe* I read of the minor wonders of nature...the sticklebacks that haunted the most ordinary pond, the newts and toads said to lurk under every stone, and the dragonflies that flitted over the dappled surface. Not, so far as I could see, in Leeds.

Alan Bennett

Science education is universally agreed to be important. There are plenty of appealing ideas around about how to do it, some of which have been espoused, at considerable expense, by education systems around the world. Yet students' accomplishments remain poor. Even many of the 'successes' only acquire an understanding that is shallow and brittle; and the majority are more bemused than empowered, more turned off science than turned on to it. Why should this be? The next three chapters try to uncover some of the assumptions that lie behind current thinking about science education, and to see to what extent they form a sound basis for planning. Are we making reasonable assumptions about the learning powers and directions of students? Are we setting ourselves (and the students) goals that are compatible and achievable? Are we conveying a true image of what science is? And – in this chapter – are we estimating accurately the extent to which learning in science can be expected to pay off in terms of a better ability, on the part of all students, to handle problems and predicaments that crop up in their out-of-school, everyday lives? Are we setting high enough standards for science education to reach; or are we, on the contrary, asking of it more than it can deliver?

## WHAT IS A PROBLEM?

Much of the modern rhetoric of science education plays on its potential –

its unique potential, one might sometimes be forgiven for inferring – for equipping young people to think in a disciplined and analytical fashion in their out-of-school and post-school lives. The claim is that this is available not just to some young people, but potentially to all; and that the residue that science lessons will leave in their minds is transferable and applicable beyond the bounds of activities that are formally 'scientific'. Science education will help you 'solve problems', 'formulate hypotheses', 'collect and analyse observations', 'carry out investigations', and so on. In the drive to free scientific skills and methods from the traditional topics and contents of the school curriculum, they seem sometimes to have become disconnected from any content at all. Science education, we are told, is capable of training the mind, of furnishing it with a powerful tool-kit of general purpose 'process skills' for thinking and learning.

But is real-life problem solving any more than a very understandable piece of wishful thinking: an expression of hope that science teaching may be of benefit to all students, non-academic as well as scholarly, rather than a well-defined and realistic programme of education? To answer this we have to delve below the surface of the slogans, and ask some hard questions – such as: what are real-life problems? To what kinds of predicament are we referring when we use this expression? Here, for example, are some of the questions that have occurred recently in my 'real life':

Why won't my motorbike start?
Is that pile of bricks in the Tate Gallery really 'art'?
What would this recipe be like if I used Cherry Brandy instead of rum?
Is it more expensive to boil a mug of water in the kettle or the microwave?
Where shall we go house-hunting, and what kind of place do we want?
Can you really eat woodlice?
Can I get rid of that funny purple patch in the corner of the TV screen?
What is the truth about the costs and risks of nuclear power?
Can you clean a swimming pool if the filter isn't working?
Why does this tin of baked beans roll so much more slowly down a slope than a same size and weight tin of Ambrosia Creamed Rice?
How can we get the dog to stop barking at imaginary cats?
Is a re-unified Germany a danger to the stability of Europe?
Should my friends let their teenage daughter set her own 'curfew' times?
How assertive shall I be in my negotiations with a prospective employer?
How should I respond to my partner's request that I put up with her being moody, grumpy and irrational when she is feeling unwell?
Is it really necessary to go into town this afternoon?

Do these fall into recognisably different types of problem, some of which require, or are amenable to 'scientific' types of 'problem solving' – and if so how? It does not seem to me that things are so conveniently tidy. Many, perhaps all, of these concerns have a potential scientific angle to them; but few, if any, demand a scientific type of solution. Whether I can fix the TV, or get the bike to start, for example, are just as much questions about my self-image, experience, expertise and priorities, as they are about the 'science' of the problem. If I am busy and can afford it, a perfectly acceptable solution is to call someone in. Whether I should be worried about Germany might partly depend on my understanding of weaponry, but such knowledge is useless without a wider frame of reference that also includes historical, geographical, political and economic considerations. My friends could, I suppose, think about their daughter's safety at night purely in terms of the statistics that relate to traffic accidents in the young adult group, or the risks of pregnancy or assault. But they are as likely to take into account their estimate of her emerging maturity, their values and beliefs as parents, and what they know of her friends. Whether, and to what extent, 'real-life problem solving' could plausibly be aided by knowledge of the kinetic theory of gases, or experience of wiring up simple electrical circuits, are by no means easy questions to deal with. Certainly we may not presume straightforward answers to them. The kind of thinking and learning that science education might be expected to foster may range in its importance from major and vital, through to minor and optional, depending not only on the problem, but also on the problem solver. And it will invariably be embedded in a personal context that involves values and preferences, aptitudes and priorities, as much as scientific knowledge or modes of thought.

One of the things that characterises problem solving in professional domains is the existence of a developing body of 'case-law'.[1] A doctor, a lawyer or an industrial chemist approaches new problems by attempting to classify them. The domain in which they work is organised around problem types and precedents, so that often the new problem can be successfully treated as another case of something known – a case of measles, or libel, or overheating in the fractionation column. Without some such typology, it is very hard to mobilise what you know. But of what 'cases' does real-life problem solving consist? It is impossible to say, largely because it is such an all-inclusive concept that it does not give one a useful handle on anything. If science education is to develop a sound rationale in terms of equipping young people to act better in their everyday lives, it will have to be much more precise about what exactly it means. At the moment the rhetoric expresses a wish rather than a way.

## WHAT IS A SCIENTIFIC REAL–LIFE PROBLEM?

Despite the fact that it seems difficult to tie scientific ways of thinking down to a specific class of real world problems, it may be possible to typify the situations where 'the scientific method' in its most traditional form works, and those where it does not. The classical scientific experiment – the cornerstone of the Popperian process of conjecture and refutation which we shall examine in more detail in the next chapter – contrives a situation in which one or a small number of so-called independent variables are systematically varied, all others are held constant, and the effect of the variations on one or a small number of other variables, the dependent ones, is measured and recorded. These observations are then compared with values that would be expected to occur if a certain combination of conjectures held good, and the conjectures are appraised and modified in the light of the kind and extent of any departures from the predictions. If Hooke's Law holds good, then the length of a spring (dependent variable) should increase in direct proportion to the weight (independent variable) hung on the end of it. If this metal is what we think it is, then it should react with dilute acid but not with water alone.

Such a way of thinking works best when the situation you are investigating can be adequately described as a closed system of a small number of independently-specifiable interacting variables. You can treat your conical flask as a self-contained world, within which the behaviour of pure chemicals is subject only to their own natures and the stimuli that you submit them to: heat, light, radiation, pressure and so on. If this micro-world were unpredictably affected also by the Dow Jones Share Index, the amount of small change in your trouser pocket, the state of the tide in Singapore and hundreds of other variables, known, unknown and un-knowable, then chemistry would become impossibly difficult. That is one reason why psychology is such a precarious science: put people under the microscope and they are influenced by just such a host of factors. The more the system you are puzzled by departs from this ideal type, the more likely the methods of conventional science are to oversimplify and misrepresent it. (It is possible to build a science of such 'open systems', so-called, but this endeavour is still in its infancy, and it looks as if it is going to grow into a very different-looking kind of enterprise.[2])

Now some of the problems that people meet in everyday life are amenable to the scientific approach. Take the example of fault-finding in an internal combustion engine again. This is a closed system of small numbers of independent, interacting variables. If the engine fails to fire, then there are only two possible reasons: no spark, or no fuel. No spark means a dead battery, a loose lead, a dirty distributor, a dud coil or cracked spark plug. Each of these 'conjectures' then indicates its appropriate 'refutation'. Each possible cause can be tested, and gradually, inevitably, the trouble is identified. But what would happen if engines could also 'play up' because they were in a bad mood, or had a headache, or wanted more pocket-money, or were hurt because you had been for a ride in another car? Or for some ephemeral and inscrutable mixture of all these, and half-a-dozen other reasons? Then the neat logic of hypothetico–deductive thinking begins to fail you, and you may be better off adopting some other, less tightly worked-out, kind of approach, like leaving it alone for a while, or sending it a bunch of flowers. These too could be described as sort-of experiments, but of a much more loose-weave, intuitive kind than those of the chemist.

But many real-life predicaments are somewhere in the middle: they are best tackled not by such a strong version of the Scientific Method, but nevertheless in a rational–empirical manner. Whether a new pair of jeans will 'run' or not is best decided by soaking the bottom of one leg in hot water before putting them in the washing machine. How long a journey will take may be best discovered with the aid of a large-scale map, a piece of string and some plausible assumptions about the state of the traffic. Others succumb better to a purely logical train of thought, a quiet period of meditation, a heart-to-heart with a trusted friend, or a couple of lessons from the pro. Part of the job of science education might be to exercise the ability to sift questions into those where hypothetico–deductive thinking is appropriate and those where it is not. Yet the cut-and-dried approach prevents young people from learning how to do so. Under pressure to cover a syllabus and to prepare for external assessments, the time to spend in such ill-defined states of inquiry is foregone, and some of the vital habits of thought on which everyday learning, as well as more formal scientific expertise, must depend remain undeveloped.

Thus the more that school science presents or exemplifies the view that science proceeds only or predominantly by a rigorous, recursive process of theorising and testing, the more it restricts its utility to a narrow subset of all possible real-life problems. And the less it addresses the issue of where its methods are applicable *and where they are not*, the more it is likely to leave by default an inaccurate or hazy sense of that utility in students' heads. If it merely leaves a vague belief that *all* 'problems' are solvable by the appliance of science, then it only takes a few experiences to the contrary to leave an equally vague sense of disillusion.

### DOES LEARNING DIFFUSE OUT OF THE LAB?

The very nature of the claims for real-life utility might give us pause: the history of the school curriculum seems to show that subjects tend to present themselves as 'a training for the mind' when they feel under threat. A delightful lampoon by Harold Benjamin called 'The sabre-tooth curriculum', published in 1939, takes us back to the earliest subjects in the curriculum: training of young people in the arts of grabbing fish, clubbing woolly horses, and scaring sabre-tooth tigers away with fire. The question was: what was to happen to these revered subjects when someone invented fishing rods, the woolly horses moved on to higher ground and were replaced by more speedy antelopes, and the tigers died out and some bears moved into the vicinity? Should they not be laid to rest, or superseded by more 'relevant' studies?

> 'Don't be foolish', said the wise old men, smiling most kindly smiles. 'We don't teach fish-grabbing to grab fish; we teach it to develop a generalised agility which can never be developed by mere training. We don't teach horse-clubbing to club horses; we teach it to develop a generalised strength in the learner which he can never get from so prosaic and specialised a thing as antelope-snare-netting. We don't teach tiger-scaring to scare tigers; we teach it for the purpose of giving that noble courage which carries over into all the affairs of life and which can never come from so base an activity as bear-killing.'

> All the radicals were silenced by this statement, all except the one who was most radical of all. He felt abashed, it is true, but he was so radical that he made one last protest.

> 'But – but anyway,' he suggested, 'you will have to admit that times have changed. Couldn't you please *try* these other more up-to-date activities? Maybe they have *some* educational value after all?'

> Even the man's fellow radicals felt that this was going a little too far.

> The wise old men were indignant. Their kindly smiles faded. 'If you had any education yourself,' they said severely, 'you would know that the essence of true education is timelessness. It is something that endures through changing conditions like a solid rock standing squarely and firmly in the middle of a raging torrent. You must know that there are some eternal verities, and the sabre-tooth curriculum is one of them!'[3]

One might tentatively propose Claxton's Law, which states that the grandiosity of a subject's rationale is inversely related to the felt security of its teachers. It is a general feature of these claims, though one that is particularly ironic in the case of science, that they are unsupported by any empirical proof of the transferability or the lay utility of the abilities claimed. As far as I know, there is no evidence at all that science education produces such real-world benefits, nor that the amount of science studied is correlated with the degree of practical nous, or analytical ability, or whatever you like, that students display in their private lives.[4]

Without such direct evidence, we are driven to arguing on *a priori* grounds, and there are good *a priori* reasons to suppose that such transfer and generalisation will *not* occur, except under very carefully created conditions. If science education is to meet the challenge of empowering students to deal better with everyday life, then it has to find a form of teaching that ensures that what has been learnt in school actually helps in the spontaneous, interwoven, value-laden world outside. Even if we identified abilities that would be of potential value out-of-school, and found ways of reliably developing them in lessons, there would still remain the crucial question of whether each ability actually came to mind when it was needed.

Recent research seems to show quite clearly one of the factors on which the 'portability' of learning depends is the overall similarity between the total situation of learning and that in which the learning is to be used: the context of retrieval. The greater the disparity, in any respect, between the two situations, the greater the risk that the functional connection will not be made, and that what in the person's mind may be of potential use stays dormant and inactive.[5] In this section, I want to explore some of the many, and from this point of view vital, differences between the contents, contexts, purposes and activities of the school science laboratory on the one hand, and the world, insofar as it can be characterised at all, of real-life learning and problem solving on the other. We shall see that 'lab-land' seems to be almost deliberately constructed to ensure that the barrier between school and outside is as impermeable as possible, and that very little flows across it at all.

### Dangerous

In terms of its appearance, the school science laboratory is, we might say, 'light-years' away from the real world. Young people are transported to a land where the familiar operation of heating things up becomes something that needs new and special kinds of equipment, with funny names, and which they are constantly being told is dangerous. What are people who have been boiling kettles, chopping vegetables, plugging and unplugging electrical appliances, frying eggs and washing up for years, to make of this world in which all these kinds of operations are treated as unprecedented, highly technical, and demanding of great skill and caution? What is motivated by the school's concern for safety, and fear of reprisal if it fails to take its *loco parentis* responsibilities seriously enough, comes across to the students as attitudes and rituals that seem to signal a different kind of world altogether. Heating a beaker of water over a Bunsen burner is clearly not the same as boiling a kettle: it is quite a tricky operation, one that requires an apprenticeship under the watchful eye of an expert, and the constant wearing of purpose-built protection, and the tying-back of hair.

### Special

Having no 'cookers' and 'kettles', the laboratory lacks also jugs, pans and bottles, oven-gloves, scales and food processors, knives and teaspoons. Students find instead test-tubes and conical flasks, scalpels and spatulas, bell-jars and centrifuges, balances and measuring cylinders, porcelain crucibles, Petri dishes and (my favourite) deflagrating spoons. Even the water taps and the electric plugs are special shapes and sizes. There are no lids, only bungs; no 'squeezy things', only tongs. These names, they will discover, are very important, and must be spelt correctly. Students will perhaps be reassured that science is, as they hoped it would be, full of weird and wonderful language – not quite 'pan-galactic gargleblasters' or 'infra-sonic hyperdrives', but close – yet puzzled that these mysterious terms turn out to apply to objects and processes that are rather mundane. They will not be told *why* familiar functions have to be carried out in unusual ways (except in terms of 'safety'), and if they are, it will usually be too soon in their scientific careers for them really to see the point, and they will probably forget.

## *Implausible*

Stranger by far than this hi-tech approach to cutting, mixing and even smelling (chemists have their own esoteric way of smelling a test-tube: you do not sniff it, but waft its aroma towards a nose placed a cautious distance away), are the implausible or impossible phenomena with which Lab-Land abounds. Students learn to talk matter of factly about pulleys which have no friction, ropes which have no weight, straight lines which have no width and solids which are mostly space; fish which are 'really' animals, wiggly lines which are 'really' straight; things that break which are 'really' liquids. They are invited into worlds where vacuums can be so perfect that feathers drop like stones, where struck balls can move for ever, where energy is never used up, and where pictures or films of the insides of animals are supposed to evoke no feeling other than keen interest.

## *Invisible*

Lab-Land is inhabited by entities which are mostly invisible and elusive. They are too small to see, or too abstract to comprehend. Yet students are told that they lie behind the world of appearances, somehow causing, controlling or constituting it. There are atoms, molecules, electrons and ions; ribosomes, corpuscles, membranes and viruses; amps and ohms and 'the force of gravity'. Many of these actors in the drama of science are stranger by far than unicorns and talking pigs, but students are not allowed to treat them as myths or inventions: they are 'real' – more real indeed than the everyday world of scrambled eggs, buses and house dust. Somehow or other the laboratory can conjure up, by the practice of the 'scientific method', this invisible, ideal universe, to which real life can at best be a poor approximation. Friction is a nuisance, a perturbation in the smoother, better world of Newtonian dynamics. Substances frequently turn out to be 'impure', however clean you had thought them to be, while 'pure' things seem to have very complicated names, and live only in glass-stoppered jars. Paradoxically it is the pure things that you are not allowed to eat. And because Real Life is so entangled, impure and non-ideal, it turns out that these powerful scientific theories cannot actually help you very much when it comes to fixing your bike, cleaning paintbrushes or deciding which of the old medicines in the bathroom cabinet ought to be thrown out.

Thus Lab-Land is physically and conceptually discontinuous with the world of home and play. Though many activities occur in both settings – heating, cleaning, cutting, weighing, measuring and so on – the instruments and terminology which attend them in the laboratory seem almost purpose built to obscure their similarity.

### *Precise*

The need for precision is of course a real one. One of the characteristics of science is that many of its phenomena have to be *sought* – they must be made to happen, or to show themselves – and by and large they will not do so unless observations are meticulous or minute. Without precision much of what makes science interesting simply will not reveal itself. And thus there are many occasions when kitchen scales, carving knife and jam-jar will not do. But science students are rarely given enough time to appreciate, to discover for themselves, that this is so, when it is so, and why it is so. The laboratory with all its paraphernalia presents itself, not as something that has evolved out of a multitude of necessities, but as a *fait accompli*, a given. The bridges that lead from the jam-jar to the test-tube, the kitchen tap to the squeezy bottle of distilled water, the pen-knife to the scalpel are invisible, and so the existence of sophisticated instruments with long names is not seen as an outgrowth of everyday interests, but as evidence of an entirely separate world that has to be accepted as such, learnt about and taken on trust. It smacks more of old-fashioned Sunday School than Education for Capability.

### *Jargon*

Likewise science demands, if its questions are to become more refined, sharper concepts and a technical vocabulary. It becomes useful to divide 'eating' into 'ingestion' and 'digestion', or to distinguish heat from temperature and mass from weight. But if such refinements are presented simply as part of the status quo, 'the way scientists talk', rather than as the tools that are *needed* in order to formulate interesting ideas, then they may be learnt, they may even form the basis for building further elaborations and superstructures, but they are hanging in the air, so to speak – ungrounded and unmotivated. Students may learn what follows from such a concept, but not what led to it and underpins it, and such fluency as they gain is to that extent a fragile one.

This is why graduate scientists (and therefore science teachers) often become inarticulate, or reveal the most elementary misconceptions, when they are asked simple scientific questions that do not conform to the familiar formulae of school. Despite their sophistication, they never really had the time or the encouragement to figure such basic things out properly; they merely, over time, got used to them. It is because they do not really understand the origins and purposes of such concepts as 'energy' or 'force' that teachers become evasive and dogmatic at crucial moments, as we saw in the last chapter. They may know the legitimate ways of using these terms, and of relating them to other terms in the technical vocabulary, and be skilful at manipulating and applying them. But teaching frequently requires teachers to step outside that self-sufficient framework of expertise and to 'go back to first principles'; and this, they find, demands a different kind of understanding that they may never have had.

*Problem seeking*

As well as the jargon and the apparatus of the science lab, there are several other important differences from everyday life that militate against the transfer of knowledge from one context to the other. For example, science seems usually to go out of the way to look for things to explain. It is in the business of problem generation as well as problem solution. If you look hard enough at anything with a scientific eye, even the most mundane, unproblematic objects or occurrences, you will find something that you do not understand, and which you can therefore construe as an invitation to inquiry. How children learn language, or why objects fall, are not things that most people lose sleep over, yet they are the stuff of science. Cognitive science, the study of how the mind/brain works, is one of the most exciting, fast-moving areas of science at the moment, yet many people would have a hard time 'seeing what the problem is', and why 'they' bother. For science, everything needs explaining. One of the most sought-after outcomes of research is a new theoretical perspective, from which not only are existing questions given a satisfactory account, but also a whole new set of questions arises. Science is, and seeks to be, interminable.

In everyday life, on the other hand, things tend to require an explanation when there is something that needs doing about them. Real life responds to personal need, and problem solving is judged successful when it delivers a positive outcome: better control or a desired change. We are not entirely utilitarian, of course. People, both young and old, are also in the generation game: all forms of play and spontaneous exploration involve the deliberate seeking or construction of problems to be solved – from looking for crabs in rocky pools to playing chess to dressing up as rock stars to teasing the cat to building towers of playing cards. In that sense, there is an aspect to real-life problem solving which does mimic the professional work of pure scientific research.

But what of problem solving in Lab-Land? For many students the motivational context is very different from that found in either science or everyday. People are not working to meet personal needs, or to satisfy intellectual curiosity, but for a complicated mixture of reasons, *some of them quite unrelated to the activity in hand*. Students may be working towards a career, but be taking chemistry solely because it is an entrance requirement for a requisite further course of study. They might be struggling to understand the difference between reflection and refraction, but only because they are afraid of the teacher, or do not want to disappoint their parents. The moods created by such 'extrinsic motivations', as they have been called, are often sharply distinct from those that attend learning in the real world.[6] Solutions, when they are found, may be the occasion neither for intrinsic satisfaction, nor for gaining access to new opportunities, but for relief from anxiety, and a dollop of approval.

Whatever the students' mood, there is a pervasive sense of training, of not doing 'it' but preparing to do 'it'. But what 'it' is is not really clear, especially for the non-academic majority. Because of this lack of a clearly visible goal, both students and teachers alike tend to fall back on the only thing on the horizon that does stand out in sharp relief: The Exam. Only rarely does everyday life present us with even remotely analogous situations – driving tests and job interviews generate nerves, but recurrent nightmares about them are nothing like as common as they are about school examinations.

Incidentally, when people talk about problem solving, they are usually referring to dealing with an occurrence that arises in the course of pursuing some self-chosen goal, and which seems to pose a non-trivial barrier to the achievement, or at least the continuing pursuit, of that goal. I have never seen science education defended as a training of better players: people who are able to amuse themselves harmlessly and creatively by taking an intelligent delight in the mundane miracles of the natural world. It is usually touted as an aid to solving 'real' problems, and therefore inevitably generates a mood of earnestness and purposefulness. For many people the very idea of science will always come trailing clouds of seriousness, and it will never occur to them that it is a lot of fun as well.

An important part of the atmosphere of school science is its predestination. Investigations do not arise opportunistically, or in response to students' immediate interests, but because they are the next thing on the syllabus, and because there are predetermined learnings that 'need' to accrue. School science offers answers to questions that it would mostly not have occurred to students to ask. They can be enticed, often quite easily, into becoming involved in the study of why a tin of Baked Beans rolls so much more slowly down a gentle slope than a tin of Creamed Rice of identical size and weight.[7] But because science education has greater ambitions than 'merely' teaching young people how to amuse themselves with their brains, the intrinsic enjoyment, and implicit uncontrolled learning, is not enough. Such exercises are usually steered by the teacher towards an understanding of proper scientific concepts such as 'viscosity' and 'momentum'. Once the students have 'bitten', they are then gently (or not-so-gently) reeled in. Real-life problem solving and 'student investigations' all too often turn out to be the instruments not of broader educational aims, but of the desire to harness students' energies more firmly to the study of the concepts of the traditional science syllabus.

### Leisurely

Like informal play, pure science often appears to be a leisurely activity; one which can be pursued when nothing more urgent or threatening is happening. Scientists may be in a rush to publish the solution to a theoretical puzzle, but basically the idea is that they have as long as it takes to find it. Quality is more important than speed. And school science gives this message all the more strongly. No problem can be that pressing when its pursuit can be chopped up into predetermined hour-long chunks, and it can be dropped whenever the bell goes. When science educators talk about 'real-life problem solving' they usually have something in mind like fault finding in a car or motorcycle engine that will not start; or being able to figure out whether it will help Jenny with her stomach upset if we give her some of those left-over antibiotics. Such problems have a sense of urgency to them. We do not want to sit around all day pondering on the processes whereby a battery produces a spark, or the differences between viruses and bacteria; we need to get to work or stop the cramps. This lack of a sense of immediacy, of problem solving in real time, makes Lab-Land remote from an enormous range of everyday situations.

### General

This practical context brings up another big difference: a solution to a real-life problem is one which meets the need, or achieves the blocked goal. It is not necessarily the most profound, elegant or coherent solution. The best solution to the dead engine may be to call the AA. The best solution to the uncertainty about the drugs may be to throw them out anyway and go and consult the pharmacist in Boots. What constitutes the best answer to a real problem has to take into account the whole personal context of resources and priorities. 'Is it worth working it out from first principles?' is always a sensible question to ask. For people who can afford it, it is perfectly rational to phone the plumber to fit the new washing machine. For someone else, with different pressures and interests, it may be the perfect opportunity to master the technology of bending and jointing pipes. And it does not matter if my understanding of the electrics in a car, or the batteries in a torch, bear no relation to my understanding of the wiring in a house. I may be able to fix the car but not put in a new ring main, or vice versa. I may even be able to do both, but in blissful ignorance of the fact that my working theories are incompatible – and that both are different from what they teach in school. How to resolve the competing claims of getting-the-thing-fixed on the one hand, and grasping-the-underlying-principles on the other, is always an open question in everyday life.

In science, however, especially as it is exemplified in school, this is not an open question. Science has very definite views about what kind of answer is to be preferred. Coherence is better than '*adhocery*': one big theory is preferable to lots of little ones. Parsimony is better than complexity: a simple, elegant theory that makes few assumptions, if it does the job, is judged superior to one in which the theoretical entities have been allowed to proliferate unchecked. Consistency is better than unorthodoxy: explanations which fit within widely accepted scientific principles are held in higher regard by scientists than those that disregard those principles. That is why astrology and 'morphic resonance'[8] are treated with suspicion by the scientific community, while astronomy and 'nuclear magnetic resonance' are not.

A central part of the scientific enterprise is the search for *generality*: concepts like 'natural selection' or 'force' or 'particle' that have the power to bring unity and coherence to an apparently diverse set of phenomena. Science extracts the general from the particular, and then seeks to account for other particulars in the same general terms. New problems are analysed in terms of existing principles. Science education has followed pure science in this respect. Its curriculum has been firmly based on this model of problem solving and knowledge generation – an approach which Donald Schon has dubbed 'technical rationality'.[9]

*Neat*

Real learning, like frontier science, often presents people with situations that are messy and ill-defined. You cannot be sure quite what is what: what is relevant and what is not; what can be treated as a separate sub-problem and what is inextricably part of the whole predicament; what can reasonably be left till later and what absolutely has to be tackled right now. Frequently you do not yet know what questions to ask, or exactly how to formulate them. This is a time (if you have *got* the time) for reflection, mulling things over, toying with ideas, tentatively trying out hunches without having a real investment in them, gathering bits and pieces of information without knowing quite how, or whether, they are going to fit in. The picture slowly clarifies; some issues or influences begin to emerge as crucial, while others, ones perhaps which started out at the front of one's mind, may recede into the background. Major life decisions involving changes of residence, career or 'marital status' are usually of this sort. But so are the early stages of a large practical project, like building your own conservatory, or planning for a year's travelling abroad.

In real-life problem solving, therefore, it is often preferable, or even necessary, to let the predicament speak for itself, and to allow a sense of its idiosyncrasy to emerge, so that the solution will be tailor-made, not off-the-peg. Before solving a problem, it has first to be formulated: it has to be turned from a hazy feeling of frustration or intrigue into a well-formed picture of Things As They Are Now, Where I Want To Be, and The Way To Proceed. This vital real-world precursor to problem solving Donald Schon calls problem *setting*.

> In real-world practice, problems do not present themselves to practitioners as givens. They must be constructed from the materials of problematic situations which are puzzling, troubling or uncertain. In order to convert a problematic situation to a problem, a practitioner must do a certain kind of work. He must make sense of an uncertain situation that initially makes no sense. . .
>
> When we 'set' the problem, we select what we will treat as the 'things' of the situation, we set the boundaries of our attention to it, and we impose upon it a coherence which allows us to say what is wrong and in what directions the situation needs to be changed.

What is more, this process of defining to ourselves what the problem *is* often continues in real life to interact with the attempts to solve it. One reflects as one is going along about what one is up to, and how one is getting along, in such a way that the constitution of the problem itself may change. Many real-life problems are of an emotional nature, for example, and they sometimes drive people to seek therapeutic help. To begin with, they may frame the problem as 'I want to do something about my nerves'; but as discussions proceed, so both the goal and the process of therapy sometimes become radically altered, so that 'insight into my relationship with my step-father' comes to take precedence even over the desire to quell the anxiety. We shall return to the issue of how to educate for such flexible and reflective awareness in Chapter 5. Suffice it to note here that conventional science lessons seem to offer few opportunities for such reflection, and are founded on a very different approach to the solution of problems.

School science presents itself to students when all this difficult, messy, exploratory thinking has been done. Problems are relatively well-defined, and students are left in little doubt about what the question is, or what aspects of the problematic situation with which they are presented are relevant to the search for its solution. To 'save time', to prevent students 'reinventing the wheel', ideas and experiments come prepackaged, like supermarket cheese. All the vital work of deciding *how* to formulate a problem, and *which*, of all the possible variables, is actually relevant to its understanding, has been done behind the scenes. This has two effects. First, it deprives students of practice at dealing with foggy situations, and thereby retards the development of those skills that would help them do so. Secondly it trains students to *expect* that all this preliminary work will be done for them, by Nature, or an obliging curriculum developer, so that they lose the habit of looking at a new situation from all sides, and become used to settling impulsively for the first formulation that they can think of. Thus school science, contrary to its avowed intent, must bear its share of the blame for the lack of sound thinking in the school-leaving population. The survey of real-life reasoning ability in America, to which I referred in Chapter 1, found that:

> Once the reasoner has evolved a simple mental model with no ostensible flaws, he or she is not likely to critique the model deliberately or consider alternative models. It is as though the reasoning process was driven primarily by an effort to minimise cognitive load and cognitive dissonance rather than by epistemic criteria.[10]

'Epistemic criteria' are those which relate to the truth of knowledge, or the validity of argument.

Similar disabilities have been noted also by the Assessment of Performance in Science Unit, in their report on 15-year-olds.[11] On page 58 it discusses results on the 'skill' of describing similarities and differences. It says:

> Pupils rarely explore the full range of possibilities when describing similarities and differences, being satisfied with two or three observations when there were many more available for description and often when many more than two or three were specifically requested.

From the point of view of real-life problem solving, as the authors quite rightly imply, this could often be dysfunctional. So why should it be?

> Pupils are probably used to directing their focus on a single variable in a relationship, since illustrative experiments in their classroom learning experience have been used to pinpoint the effect of, say, mass or length on pendulum periodicity. It could well be that pupils have been positively discouraged to [sic]

gather data other than those central to the concept being studied, since the description of other variables may be seen to divert pupils and detract from their ability to understand the key relationship.

And of course we do not need to ask who it is that has decided which variable is, at that moment, 'key'.

Lack of practice in designing their own investigations from scratch also compounds the problem, raised above, of failure to appreciate for themselves the need for precision in measurement. There is a big difference, for example, between being able to use an electronic balance, and knowing when and why it is useful to ascertain the weight of something so precisely. When investigations are carefully designed for students, the effect may be to give practice in such technical skills, but at the expense of developing a spontaneous feel for their sphere of utility.

*Cerebral*

In general, science education seems to follow science proper in paying more attention to the quality of the explanation than the availability of practical pay-offs. Of course professional engineers, metallurgists and pharmaceutical researchers are very interested in practical solutions to problems, but the image of science that predominates in school is still of the slow, inexorable accumulation of deep understanding. There may be films and demonstrations about the search for an anti-AIDS drug, or the operation of a foetal heart monitor, or the building of the Channel Tunnel; but then it is back to 'the facts' about genetic inheritance, electromagnetic induction and the reactivity series of metals. Science is presented more as a network of ideas and procedures, an intellectual unravelling of the secrets of nature, than as the search for solutions to human problems.

This tension mirrors the familiar one between 'pure' and 'applied' science. What directs the course of research: is it Nature leading us from question to question, on the basis of the answers she gives; or is it human need and purpose that drives the inquiry? School science, in so far as it gives any sense of science as evolving over time, tends to convey the image of science as 'pure' research, and thereby to reinforce the idea that *explanation* is primary, and *exploitation* of theory for human benefit – for the solving of human problems – is secondary. Pure science, in this picture, is constantly asking 'why?' and 'how come?' and 'what if?'. (The current emphasis in some countries on 'technology' as a complement to 'science' goes a variable way to redressing this balance; but there is a danger – to the extent that technology is presented as a separate subject – of leaving science looking even more 'academic' by contrast.)

But as we have seen, this is a very different attitude from the one that informs much of our real-life problem solving. There is not the time or the

energy, often, to keep on asking 'why?', because the question 'so what?' is
breathing down your neck, or because the need is not great enough to
warrant the investment of effort. A satisfactory explanation is one which tells
you what you want to know, and only as much as you want to know. (There
is an old story about a little girl who went to find her mother and asked her,
'Mummy, how do traffic lights work?' Her mother, who was busy, replied,
'I don't know, dear. Why don't you go and ask your father?' To which the
girl responded, 'Oh, I don't want to know *that* much about it.')

Thus if students are to be inducted into the ways of science, and are to
be able to use that induction to their everyday benefit, they need to develop
an appreciation of why 'why?' is such a useful question: why it is sometimes
valuable to put the pressing demands of problem solving on one side and
pursue interesting puzzles for their own sake. If there were the opportunity
for them to discover that more time spent in inquiry and speculation
sometimes produced better answers to practical questions, that 'the long
way round could turn out to be the shortest way home', then a bridge
would have been built between the laboratory and everyday life. But here
again the link is usually not made, and another discontinuity is created.

## *Justifying*

Because of its emphasis on the *internal* quality of science, rather than its
practical pay-offs, school science places great value on the justification and
communication of ideas. Its assessment, for example, is still very much in
terms of an intellectual grasp of concepts, and an ability to articulate ideas
and justify conclusions. Students' understanding of meteorology is tested
by written questions on clouds, land formations, air currents and precipitation, not by counting the number of rainy afternoons on which they
failed to bring their anoraks to school. In the world of real-life, real-time
problem solving, it does not usually matter how you got there; the question
is, does it work? You may be called upon to share your invention or
solution, and to explain how it operates; but it is not very often that people
are required to lay out, in a nice logical sequence, the steps by which they
got there. It is quite common that they have not the faintest idea where
their ideas came from. But that is not the issue. The proof of the pudding
is not in the recipe but in the eating.

In school science, as in school maths, however, it is no use being
intuitive, or making guesses, however educated they might be. You have
to be able to 'show your working', to explain in a clear and logical fashion
*why* you think what you think. The present enthusiasm for discussion in
science lessons – for getting students to be explicit about their scientific
conceptions and to work out their implications by talking to each other –
reinforces still further the idea that science is nothing if not communicable,

and that the process of scientific discovery, as well as of dissemination, relies on explicit, rational, logical, defensible trains of thought and of language. We shall return to discuss later whether this premium on rationality and articulacy is a 'good thing' or not. Here all I am pointing out is another important way in which the ethos of school science marks it off from the world of everyday life.

### Authoritarian

School science is different from real-life problem solving in adding another criterion for judging the value or correctness of an idea: the approval of an authority, in the shape of the teacher or the textbook. The routine work of scientific research laboratories, too, relies to an extent on the judgements of professors, journal referees and the like: as we shall see in the next chapter 'real' science is by no means free of such personal arbitration. But generally speaking people in science become authorities on the basis of their accomplishments: their power and status is a reflection of the respect in which they are held by their peers. And the acid test ought at least to continue to be the quality of the work they produce. In school science, however, the authoritative (and authoritarian) role for the teacher seems pre-eminent, and it is based purely on the office the teachers hold, and not on their ability to advance the subject which they are attempting to profess.

It is the teacher, or the textbook, which turns out in the end to be the arbiter of students' performance, not the natural consequences of their skill in inquiry. The commonplace experience of the post-Nuffield science student is of 'experiments' that the teacher presented as true investigations, but which invariably turned out, if you waited long enough, to have a particular sought-after observation or solution. Even despite their best intentions, teachers have continued to operate as the checkers and validators of results and conjectures.

### Problems and their social context

The final area in which school science and real-life problem solving might be said to differ is in the social context which surrounds each of them. In the everyday world, learning is often, though not always, a social activity. People gather together to explore issues and challenges of common concern; or they ask each other for help. Social groups are constituted on the basis of mutual interests, or of pre-existing relationships within which mutual support can be expected. The world of real science is also an essentially social one. Scientists commonly work in teams – it is not unusual to see a paper in a physics journal authored by twenty people or more. And without communication and discussion the march of science could not proceed.

Traditionally school science on the other hand has been seen as rather a solitary enterprise, with students making their own discoveries and developing their understanding of the presented concepts as best they can. Since Nuffield, though, two shifts have taken place which have moved the laboratory context somewhat closer to the outside world. First the increased use of practical work – coupled with the fact that there is rarely enough equipment for students to work on their own – has meant that science lessons have inevitably become more social occasions. And secondly science educators have begun to realise that, whatever the form of organisation of the lesson, students *are* social beings, and their developing understandings of science are going to reflect the societies and groups in which they take part. Despite these changes in attitude, however, the *nature* of the social relationships in a science lesson remains very different from those that emerge spontaneously to organise students' informal problem solving outside lesson time. In the latter case, there is no designated teacher (though the *role* of teacher may be adopted by individuals for particular purposes), no prescribed time structure, no requirements to complete what has been started, no test other than personal satisfaction.

### A bridge too far?

In his book *Learning Science*, the Australian science educator Dick White says: 'If a substantial proportion of laboratory investigations used common materials instead of things never encountered elsewhere, the gap (between school and everyday) would be bridged.'[12] What I have tried to argue in this chapter is that there are a great many ways in which the school lab differs from out-of-school learning and problem-solving contexts; and consequently that it would take much more than just the importation into the lab of some familiar materials to link the two worlds. White's hope is a fond one. While it would be a start to show how scientific methods and attitudes could be brought to bear on everyday objects, it would not be any more than that.

This chapter has looked in some detail at the claim that science education could be set up so as to enhance young people's real-life problem-solving ability. What we have discovered is that this, in anything like the present school context, is an unlikely possibility. First, it turns out that we do not yet have anything like a clear enough idea of what it is that we are aiming to enhance. And secondly, there are so many ways in which the whole set-up of school differs from the informal contexts of everyday life, that it is unlikely that *whatever* we achieve in science lessons is going to make very much impact on natural competence in the real world. We have to conclude at the moment that such claims and justifications for science education are too ill-defined, and too grandiose; and that the impermeable membrane separating school from home has not yet been breached with any sustained success.[13]

NOTES

[1] This discussion follows that of Donald Schon in *The Reflective Practitioner*, Basic Books: New York, 1983.

[2] See Erich Jantsch, *The Self-Organising Universe*, Pergamon: Oxford, 1980; Ilya Prigogine and Isabelle Stengers, *Order out of Chaos*, Heinemann: London, 1984.

[3] Harold Benjamin, 'The sabre-tooth curriculum', in J.A. Pediwell, *The Sabre-Tooth Curriculum*, McGraw-Hill: New York, 1939.

[4] See D. N. Perkins, 'Post-primary education has little impact on informal reasoning', *Journal of Educational Psychology*, **77**, 562–71, 1985.

[5] J. Eich, 'The cue-dependent nature of state dependent retrieval', *Memory and Cognition*, **8**, 157–73, 1980; E. Tulving, *Elements of Episodic Memory*, OUP: Oxford, 1983.

[6] The 'intrinsic/extrinsic' distinction is explained in my *Live and Learn*, Harper and Row: London, 1984; reissued Open University Press: Milton Keynes, 1989, Chapter 2. It was first popularised by Jerome Bruner in *Towards a Theory of Instruction*, Belknap Press: Cambridge MA, 1967.

[7] This example is beautifully elaborated by A. A. Hyde and M. Bizar, *Thinking in Context: Teaching cognitive processes across the elementary school curriculum*, Longman: New York, 1989.

[8] The concept used by Rupert Sheldrake to explain the putative fact that innovative solutions to problems somehow communicate themselves around the world without any direct contact between the individuals or societies involved. See his *A New Science of Life* , Anthony Blond: London, 1985.

[9] Schon, *op. cit.*

[10] Perkins, *op. cit.*

[11] Assessment of Performance Unit, *Science at Age 15*, HMSO: London, 1988.

[12] Richard White, *Learning Science*, Blackwell: Oxford, 1988.

[13] For further reading on the way in which mental skills are tied to specific tasks and contexts, I suggest a pair of excellent articles from the journal *Educational Researcher*, vol. **18**, January/February 1989. They are 'Are cognitive skills context-bound?', by David Perkins and Gavriel Salomon, pp. 16–25; and 'Situated cognition and the culture of learning', by John Seely Brown, Allan Collins and Paul Duguid, pp. 32–41. The same questions are explored by Jean Lave in her *Cognition in Practice*, CUP: Cambridge, 1988. For a very readable account of pioneering experimental work on this issue with younger children, and its implications for education, see Margaret Donaldson's renowned *Children's Minds*, Fontana: London, 1987. Donald Schon's *The Reflective Practitioner*, *op. cit.*, and the sequel *Educating the Reflective Practitioner*, Jossey-Bass: San Francisco, 1987, explore the extent to which problem solving is situation-specific in the world of professionals such as architects, therapists. . .and teachers.

# CHAPTER FOUR

·

# THE NATURE OF SCIENCE PROPER

The stumbling way in which even the ablest of scientists in every generation has had to fight through thickets of erroneous observations, misleading generalisations, inadequate formulations and unconscious prejudice is rarely appreciated by those who obtain their scientific knowledge from textbooks.

James B. Conant

In the course of the discussion of the differences between problem solving as it is presented in the school science lab, and as it occurs spontaneously in everyday life, I have remarked in several places on the way in which school science is also distinct, in its overt and its hidden curriculum, from 'real science'. Before we can decide what science education should be, we need to know the options it has available for presenting or conveying the nature of science. And we also need to identify clearly what images it has, wittingly or unwittingly, been presenting; and which images are the most suitable for young people to absorb. As we shall see, there is now acknowledged to be a big gap between the way scientists actually work, and the idealistic caricatures that have sometimes been presented of scientific knowledge and 'the scientific method'. But the question remains of the extent to which it is necessary and appropriate for secondary school (let alone primary) students to be introduced to the complex warts-and-all world of real scientific activity.

There is also the question of whether the nature of science should be addressed explicitly, made an object of study in its own right, or whether an image of science is better conveyed by practice, example and demonstration. And if the former, at what age might students be expected to be able to undertake this conscious analysis. The National Science Curriculum for England and Wales, for example, has taken a clear stand on these two issues. The Nature of Science is to be addressed explicitly: it now has its own 'attainment target'. And it is to start at 'level 4', which is roughly the start of secondary school. At this age, students should 'be able to give an account of some scientific advance. . .describing the new ideas and investigation or invention. . .'. Later on they should 'be able to explain how a scientific explanation from a different culture or a different time contributes to our present understanding'; 'understand the uses of evidence and the tentative nature of proof'; and 'be able to relate differences in scientific opinion to the uncertain nature of scientific evidence'. As Robin Millar says in the introduction to his book *Doing Science*, 'the general idea that science education should include some explicit treatment of the nature of science is widely acknowledged, at least at the level of science education rhetoric.' He also notes, however, the danger of such an explicit treatment being undermined by the image that is embedded in students' day-to-day experience of science lessons. 'Piecemeal attempts to "tag on" a few lessons or activities dealing overtly with the nature of science may achieve very little, if they ignore the implicit messages about the nature of science which are being communicated all the time.'[1] It is to these questions that we shall have to return once we have surveyed some of the insights that have been generated by work in the philosophy and sociology of science.

To ask what science is, is to ask not one but several questions. If one tries to answer them all at the same time, as people frequently have during the course of the last three hundred years, one ends up in a dreadful tangle, having answered none of them satisfactorily. In this chapter I am therefore going to proceed more cautiously, and take them one at a time. In the order in which I shall look at them, the questions are:

What is the nature of scientific knowledge?
How is scientific knowledge generated?
What does it take to be a good scientist?
How is scientific knowledge evaluated and accredited?

Before we start on the 'true' nature of science, however, it would be useful to put these discussions in context by making a few comments on the more naive view that students, and perhaps their teachers too, have picked up from the world at large.

THE PUBLIC IMAGE OF SCIENCE

The disparities between what a critical analysis shows that scientists are doing, and what the public suppose them to be doing, may be quite wide. In the public mind there are a number of common attributes that make an activity appear scientific, whether it is or not in fact. We are not here talking about society's definition of science so much as a range of facets or 'symptoms' whose presence, in increasing numbers and intensities, lead people to diagnose an activity as 'scientific'. First, activities are more likely to be thought of as scientific if they relate to the physical world, rather than to the world of human affairs. Physics and chemistry are the prototypical sciences; botany and ethology somewhat less so; and psychology, sociology and economics are clearly suspect as sciences at all – as witnessed by the British Government's insistence on changing the name of the main research funding agency from the 'Social Science Research Council' to the 'Economic and Social Research Council'. And despite the fact that the kinds of thought they use overlap with science quite considerably, subjects like history or literary criticism are not popularly thought of as scientific at all.

Second, things look more scientific if they are concerned with numbers and measurement. 'The average family has 2.4 children' feels more of a scientific statement than 'The average family has a couple of kids'. An advertisement that tells you that '9 out of 10 owners who expressed a preference' chose a certain cat food plays on the tendency to attribute a science-like status to statements that are quantified. They invite us to form images of people in white coats with clip-boards busily ascertaining 'the facts'. Third, measurements and observations look more scientific if they are made with the aid of machines that rely on sophisticated technology and are very expensive. They are good if they have names like 'electron microscope' or 'cyclotron', or even better if the names are so complicated that you can only call them by letters like a CAT scanner, or an ECG machine.

Fourth, language has a scientific feel to it if it is peppered with special purpose hieroglyphics and equations like '$E = mc^2$', and mysterious entities like Black Holes, Antimatter and DNA. And fifth, you can recognise science because it is very hard to understand and has to be explained to you, usually by people (traditionally men, though this is changing) who wear dull clothes and are less concerned than average about their personal appearance. If you asked for a scientist from Central Casting, you would be much more likely to get Max von Sydow than Tom Cruise, and either than Elizabeth Taylor or Whoopi Goldberg – though you might just get Sigourney Weaver in spectacles. (Remember, we are talking of stereotypes here. Science is no more necessarily male than it is numerical or physical. Yet of such impressions is its public image constituted.)

In summary, activities tend to be treated as scientific, and accorded a particular respect, if they wear what are really only the accoutrements of science. Precision measurements and technical vocabularies have developed in order to refine and sharpen the way science is carried out, but they do not constitute its essence, any more than an array of scalpels can be taken to sum up surgery. In order to see what needs to be done to counteract such misapprehensions through science education, we need to identify more clearly what science is at its core.

## WHAT ARE THE NATURE AND STATUS OF SCIENTIFIC KNOWLEDGE?

Answers to this fundamental question have progressed through many different stages over the course of the last 300 years, and been the cause of much debate. All I can do here is to boil this corner of the history of ideas down to an outline that is inevitably a caricature, but which nevertheless, I hope, retains some of the main elements of the way in which thinking about science, as well as science itself, has changed. The simplest, and earliest, idea about scientific knowledge is that it just arises if one listens carefully enough to the voice of Nature. This 'induction' view was first associated with Francis Bacon, writing at about the start of the seventeenth century, not a scientist himself, but trying to make sense of the new world of empirical investigation that was emerging around him. Scientific knowledge, he proposed, consisted of 'facts' and 'laws'. It was the scientists' job to observe Nature carefully, to collect observations, and to sift them for the generalities and patterns which they contained, as gold prospectors panned their gravel for 'pay-dirt', or bees painstakingly manufacture honey from millions of individual flowers. Doing an experiment was deliberately going and looking for more 'facts' that would support, or weaken, a candidate law or generalisation. Science discovers truths about the world, and scientific knowledge consists of those general statements that have passed the test of sufficient observation.

Now there are several obvious difficulties with this. First, no amount of observation, however accurate and painstaking, can ever justify us in moving a candidate generalisation from the category 'probable' into the category 'proven beyond all possible doubt'. However many white swans you may have seen, the possibility of a black one, lurking round the next corner, waiting to wreck your life's work, can never be ruled out. No matter how many cups you have made at home, the generalisation 'boiling water makes good tea' is going to fall apart as you pump up your Primus stove on the top of Everest.

Secondly, it is just not true that all science consists of is general statements and descriptive laws. Yes, there is good old Boyle's Law, telling us that the volume of a fixed mass of gas at constant temperature is inversely proportional to the pressure exerted on it. Yes, there is the general observation that animals that lay eggs do not suckle their young. Both of these statements have their 'black swans' (or their duck-billed platypuses) but they do hold quite widely. But science is also full of lots of *ideas*: theories and explanations that are designed to get below the surface of things and tell us how they came to be, what makes them tick, and, most importantly of all, how they are likely to behave in the future. And these theories abound with hypothetical influences and invisible entities that nobody has ever observed at all – quarks, gravity, volts, momentum, the unconscious mind, the Big Bang, continental drift, and millions of others. We may interpret the movement of a dial *in terms of* volts, or a slip of the tongue as being *evidence for* the unconscious, but neither of these creatures has ever looked at anyone across the top of its morning newspaper and said 'hello'.

So the second view proposes that scientific knowledge consists of *two* kinds of things, facts and theories. On the one hand there are, as Bacon said, incontrovertible statements about what was so. On the other there are theories and ideas which are human creations designed to explain why and how things came to be so. This is the view that Chalmers, in his useful little book *What is this Thing Called Science?*,[2] calls 'naive instrumentalism'. This kind of distinction is enshrined in the orthodox format of the scientific report, which has separate sections for Results on the one hand – the 'facts' you have discovered – and Discussion – where you speculate about what these results *mean* – on the other. First you get the facts; then you sit down and dream up theories to account for them. The fact that school science usually teaches students to write according to this formula suggests that some such image forms the basis for the view of science which it transmits. And indeed it seems to fit very well with our common sense view of things, which distinguishes pretty clearly between 'perception' and 'conception' – seeing and thinking. Seeing is straightforward and usually reliable. Thinking is where we interpret what we have seen, and exercise our options. It is through thought that people seek to direct and control their lives, drawing on their experience and needs; not through the way they perceive.

The big problem with this distinction between fact and theory, seeing and thinking, is that it does not hold water. 'Observations' and 'interpretations' are not quite different kinds of thing; they exist on a spectrum or a continuum. At one extreme there are Science Fiction entities like Martians, which are clearly, at this stage of our knowledge, creations of the human mind. Then there are 'quarks' and 'the Gaia hypothesis' (which suggests that the whole Earth acts like a living organism to regulate its own temperature and atmospheric composition). These obviously have the status at the moment of scientific conjectures, proposed but not yet established. But what about 'The heart pumps blood around the body', or 'Wires of different thicknesses have different electrical resistance', or 'Copper sulphate crystals are blue.' These seem like statements of fact to us today, rather than conjectures, yet they are not nearly as straightforward as they look. Three hundred and fifty years ago, when William Harvey proposed (note, 'proposed') the then novel idea that the heart was a pump, this did not seem like a self-evident fact at all: it was a startling hypothesis that it took some years for people to come to accept. It is a fact to us that the Earth and the other planets in the solar system rotate around the sun. To intelligent churchmen in the sixteenth century, who were by no means as stupid and bigoted as the textbooks would have us believe, the idea was preposterous – and they had good arguments for believing it to be so.

We talk casually about electrical resistance as if it were an intrinsic property of wires; yet it is equally a theoretical notion which expresses the relationship between the 'potential difference' applied to the ends of the wire, and the strength of current which then flows through it. When we say that crystals of $CuSO_4$ are blue, we are stating a 'fact' that only has meaning within the whole conceptual apparatus of 'elements', 'compounds', 'crystalline structure' and so on. When we heat it and it turns white, is our statement that 'the crystalline structure breaks down when the bound molecules of $H_2O$ are driven off as steam, leaving an anhydrous powder which does not absorb light of the same wavelengths' fact or theory? To an A level chemistry student, it might look like a fact. To a research chemist it might look like a very over-simplified, and in some respects false, theoretical proposal. And to a complete newcomer to science, it will not make any sense at all. What kind of statement it is seems to depend on who you are talking to. Things that look to one person like self-evident descriptions or observations turn out, when you start trying to justify them to someone else, to rely on a whole substructure of theory – taken-for-granted theory, but theory nonetheless. The language in which observations are recorded presupposes a view of the world that is not simply 'given'.

The 'atomic solar system' model of matter has percolated into school science text-books, and even into everyday life, and is widely treated as if it were 'true': there really are little balls of negative electricity that revolve around a tiny but very dense core in definite orbits, like the planets around the sun. Though you cannot see them, 'scientists have shown' that this is what matter is 'really' like. Here is another theory which has lost its 'as if' status, and lingers on in people's minds as the truth. The interesting thing to note about this is not that it has long been abandoned by working scientists themselves, but that even its creator, the famous Danish physicist Neils Bohr, never pretended that things inside the atom were *really* like this. It was just a way of representing some useful ideas in a way that was easy to grasp. Another of the great physicists, Werner Heisenberg, in an autobiographical reflection, described Bohr as:

> using classical mechanics or quantum theory as a painter uses his brush or colours. Brushes do not determine the picture, and colour is never the full reality; but if he keeps the picture before his mind's eye, the artist can use his brush to convey, however inadequately, his own mental picture to others. Bohr. . .[has formed] an intuitive picture of different atoms; a picture he can only convey to other physicists by such inadequate means as electron orbits and quantum conditions. It is not at all certain that Bohr himself believes that electrons revolve inside the atom.[3]

Consider this attempt by a teacher to introduce the notion of biological classification to a group of nine-year-olds. First she elicits the idea that there are basically two types of things, living and non-living. Then she continues:

> Teacher: 'Every living thing is either a – or a – (indicating the blanks non-verbally). . .Lucy, give me one division.'
> Lucy: 'People?'
> T: 'People are just part of one of the two divisions.'
> Peter: 'Plants and animals.'
> T: Good for you, Peter. That's right. Everything in this world is either plant or animal. People, Lucy, are animals, so they fit in this division.'
> L: 'People aren't animals, they're humans.'
> T: 'People are animals, the same as cats and dogs and so on.' (much laughter and several loud objections by a large number of pupils) 'People *are animals*. What's wrong with that? They're not plants, are they?'[4]

What is a 'scientific fact' to the teacher is clearly a source of both surprise and discomfort to the students – just as it still is to many people to be told that 'human beings are descended from the apes'. They are used to using the word 'animal' in a way that *contrasts* it with 'human beings' – as we all are. When you see a sign that says 'No animals allowed', do you assume that you are banned as well as your dog? Because you know that vets are people who treat sick animals, do you have difficulty choosing between them and your G.P. when your daughter breaks her leg? Of course not. The 'fact' that people are animals is *only* a fact within a certain category system, which scientists have agreed to use; and the specialised meaning of the word 'animal' is given to it by that method of categorisation. Whether people are or are not animals is not a fact of nature; it is a matter of how people consent to use the word. The world does not come pre-perforated, like toilet paper, ready to fall apart into natural concepts the moment you give it a gentle tug. It is we, scientists as well as lay people, who decide where the lines are to be drawn. Scientists are just more concerned than the rest of us to draw a map of 'reality' that is as neat, elegant, economical and consistent as possible.

So it is widely accepted now that science is fundamentally conceptual and theoretical. 'Facts' are statements about the world, cast in terms of underlying theory, which have become uncontroversial. And they are statements about *aspects* of the world that are presumed, again in terms of some set of priorities and preconceptions, to be interesting. You simply cannot go out with your notebook and a fresh pair of eyes and 'observe': as soon as you look around you, you are making, whether you know it or not, decisions about what is noteworthy, what is interesting, relevant or puzzling. Immediately the world is seen in the distorting mirror of your own interests and judgements, which highlights and magnifies some aspects, turning them into the 'foreground', and which thereby relegates other – potentially just as problematic – features to the periphery and the backdrop.

So the subsequent images of scientific knowledge have had to give a much more central role to ideas. Sir Karl Popper, the best-known proponent of the third view we shall consider, sees scientific knowledge as consisting of those ideas or 'conjectures' about reality which have been proposed, and which have not yet been shown to be inadequate by the process of experimentation.[5] Ideas can never be proved: the conjecture 'all swans are white' could be (and actually is) false, despite a lot of 'confirming' sightings of white swans. What would be much more informative would be to spot a black swan, because this definitely would show the conjecture to be false; and therefore the most productive kind of scientific activity is to look for exactly those observations which would *dis*confirm the conjecture you are interested in, and which would force you to abandon your conjecture, modify it, or make it more precise. Maybe 'all indigenous, northern hemisphere swans are white' is closer to the mark. Scientific knowledge can never, by its very nature, be certain knowledge. But nevertheless the quality of the conjectures gradually improves as those that survive the most 'tests' persist, and those that are refuted die out. The process of scientific development is like that of natural selection: survival of the fittest.

One problem with this more sophisticated view is its implicit model of what a scientific theory is like. It tends to assume that theories are relatively straightforward statements of conjecture which could be decisively disproved by the 'right' observations. My theory says A and yours says B, so we go and see which of A or B actually happens, and then one of us is shown to be wrong. Now some rather simple theories are of this form, but most of those which hold sway in contemporary science are much more complex. They are not like coconuts – one direct hit from a well-aimed experiment and they are knocked off their stand. They are more like houses that comprise a lot of bricks put together in a complicated way, and which can only be demolished brick by brick, or more commonly just abandoned.

Thus we need to move to the fourth view of scientific knowledge, one which is associated with the name of Imre Lakatos, which sees the central theories of modern science as being like large trees (see Figure 1).[6]

The roots of the tree are those assumptions which are so taken for granted, so dissolved in the way scientists think and operate, that they are very largely unconscious. These assumptions form a framework of presuppositions within which theories are developed, but which are only occasionally themselves unearthed and submitted to scientific scrutiny. In physical science, the idea that matter is made up of combinations of a limited number of 'fundamental particles' is such an assumption. Most research in nuclear physics tests ideas within this point of view; it does not

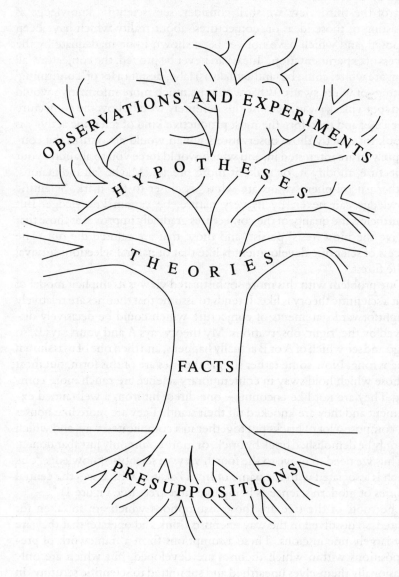

Figure 1. The tree of scientific knowledge

question the point of view itself. Likewise in neuroscience, the idea that the brain is a complicated tangle of nerve cells which constitute a vastly sophisticated biocomputer for recording and processing information, is taken as read. What is interesting about the brain, in this view, are the neurons and their interconnections. The other kinds of cells, and the extra-cellular environment, is seen as 'backdrop'; as having secondary or supportive functions which could influence the main business of the brain, but which was not itself the main business. So when someone comes along and suggests the reverse, or proposes that the brain is better viewed as a kind of 'gland', he or she will not be taken seriously by the mainstream of research scientists.[7]

This root structure furnishes the language, the perspectives and the priorities that are 'natural' for scientists to accept and adopt, when they are working in the field which it defines. The next layer up, the first 'above ground' we might say, is the 'facts' which are seen as being relevant and uncontroversial. They constitute the trunk of the tree, the conscious consensus, the stockpile of 'what everybody knows'. The brain is divided into two hemispheres. The outermost layer of the brain is the neocortex. The hindmost part of the neocortex of each hemisphere is concerned with the processes of vision. Neurons communicate at synaptic junctions by the release of neurotransmitters. And so on. Nobody bothers (at the moment) to ask questions about the brain's basic anatomical architecture – the 'existence' of forebrain, midbrain and hindbrain, temporal lobe and parietal lobe, limbic system and corpus callosum, are what we *know*.

From the top of this solid trunk of common knowledge (common to those 'in the know') can proliferate more speculative ideas – the ones which we usually recognise *as* ideas, and call 'theories'. The different 'branches' of theory sprout 'twigs' of hypotheses, and right out at the edges of the tree we find the 'leaves' of observation and experiment. How are 'concepts' and 'memories' represented in the brain, we can ask. Maybe as single cells with lots of connections to different sensory and association areas all over the cortex, like the hub of a bicycle wheel with all the spokes radiating out. Such an idea was proposed a few years ago. So this conjecture sent people off looking for such 'grandmother cells', as they were dubbed. They proved hard to find. So the alternative conjecture, that concepts existed as large networks of associations, distributed all over the brain, without any one central point where they all came together, was proposed, and this, at the moment, is one of the dominant theories.

However even such proposals as these are not readily refuted by 'crucial tests' in the Popperian style. In order to look for 'grandmother cells' one has to have acquired a great deal of technical skill in anatomy, physiology, computing – and even the physical construction of apparatus. Then one has to decide what kind of animal one is going to study; how one is going to perform the tests on it; how many tests one is going to make; what part of the brain one is going to search within; and a hundred other practical details. If one then fails to find any 'grandmother cells', there are a hundred possible reasons why, other than the fact that they do not exist. Maybe the electrodes were too large. Maybe the rat's brain works in a different way from ours. Maybe the recording equipment was not sensitive enough to pick up the crucial signals. And so on. One negative result, in real science, very rarely constitutes a decisive falsification of a clear-cut conjecture. Each experiment arises from a hypothesis that sits on top of this mountain of interwoven assumptions, some of them 'obvious', some of them 'contentious' and some of them of no real interest, but you had to assume *something* in order to make the experiment test anything at all.

## THE GENERATION OF SCIENTIFIC KNOWLEDGE

The view of the 'scientific method' that I want to present has several different levels, or layers, to it. Let me sketch these very briefly before discussing each in more detail. At its core, scientific activity relies on a certain type of thinking. This style of reasoning is by no means exclusive to science, but it is one of its essential ingredients, and science is, we might say, the fallible attempt to apply such thinking more purely and methodically than it is to be found elsewhere. At its most general, 'scientific thinking' involves an interaction between three more basic activities: observing, generating ideas, and testing ideas. The particular form that these activities take, and their relative prominence, varies quite widely across different specific fields of science, and with the different phases that any one field can find itself in.

In order to understand science proper, however, these focal activities have to be seen as going on within three surrounding rings of influence (see Figure 2.). First comes the personality and temperament of the individual scientist – the 'personal context'. Then we have to see the scientist within the context that is provided by the other scientists working in the same field, especially those of high rank. And finally there is the wider context of social pressures and political/economic decisions which impinge, however indirectly, on the work that is carried out. Without an awareness of each of these factors, it is easy to develop a lop-sided view of science, and to exaggerate either its infallibility, or its dangers.

### Scientific thinking

However we conceive of science, and however much of an overlay of social control and personal investment there may be, science is

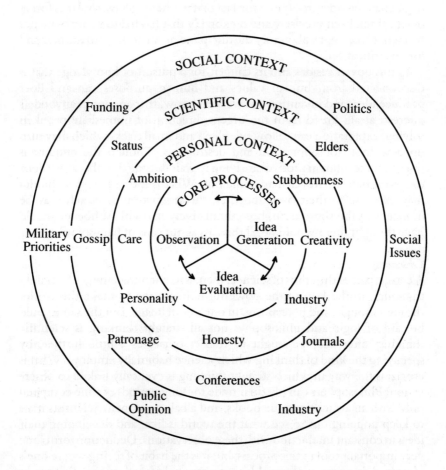

Figure 2.  The nature of scientific activity

characterised, and finally judged, by its ability to see where ideas lead, in terms of observable implications, rather than to direct them and promote them in terms of one's personal preferences. It is a general psychological 'truth' that people's actions and perceptions are channelled by their needs and desires. The power of scientific thinking lies in its commitment, fallible though it surely is, to observing and accounting for what seems to be so, regardless of whether one wishes it to be so or not. Thinking becomes at least somewhat dissociated from personal motivation, and is thereby liberated from the constraints of immediate relevance and gain. Learning can be directed by 'interests' rather than needs, and can therefore be pursued on broader fronts. It is the fact that mathematics is a tool that forces one to think both precisely and inexorably that has led so many branches of science to accept voluntarily the discipline of equations and the demand for quantification.

In this power resides also its danger, for a pursuit of knowledge that is disconnected from human values and human purposes can and does produce ideas and inventions, as we well know, that are not in anybody's interests at all. Freed from the urgent direction of immediate problem solving, exploration can follow side alleys and small tracks which may turn up new tools for oppression and destruction. Though the enquiry is dispassionate, human motives are lying in wait outside the laboratory door to appropriate whatever may come out. What is more, new possibilities may give rise to their own appetites, the satisfaction of which may be innocent in the short-term, but cumulatively harmful. Whoever would have thought there would be all this fuss about cans of hair-spray?

*Observing*

A central part of the ethos of science, then, is its encouragement of 'straight thinking', in the face of the powerful human urge to make the world, through thought and perception, in one's own image. But the same could be said of logic and philosophy: not all straight thinking is scientific thinking, after all. We ought to restrict ourselves a little further, by specifying the kind of thinking which science habitually employs. What is crucial is the way in which straight thinking is cyclically linked to obser-vation. Philosophers can ply their trade for long periods of time equipped only with an armchair, some books, and a ball-point pen. Scientists have to keep popping out to see what the world is like, and developing their ideas in constant interaction with these observations. Deduction forms one very important tool in this process; but it is the habit of seeing where one's ideas lead, in terms of observable, but not yet observed, events, that marks the scientist out from the logician or the mathematician.

But if scientists are not infallible as deducers, they are by no means perfect observers either. What they notice and record has some question, hunch or hypothesis behind it, always. What that guiding framework is may not be very well-formulated, nor very conscious, but the interest is constantly in uncovering and clarifying such glimmerings as there are. Observation is continually driven by human interest and human thought, and the less obvious the controlling hand of our preconceptions, the more important it is to remember that it is there, and to reflect constantly on what it may tacitly be directing us away from, as well as towards. The fact that data are 'contaminated' with scientists' existing beliefs and assumptions is something that they must try to be aware of, and at times to guard against. One of the big problems experienced by anthropologists, for example, is how to put aside their own cultural habits of thought while trying to understand how people who are very different from themselves view the world. And it is not just that we judge other people in terms of our own world view; the theories that we currently subscribe to – whether we know it or not – mould all our observations. What Bacon and other 'inductivists' ignored was precisely how pervasive, some would say inevitable, is this tendency to see the world in terms of the theories and beliefs you already hold.

*Evaluating*
Ideas are tested on the basis of their elegance and coherence; and on their ability to account for what is already known. But the cornerstone of the scientific method is the ability of an idea to anticipate the unknown. So the second element in the scientists' trio of core processes (those at the centre of Figure 2.) – the Popperian one – is that of deriving predictions about as yet unexplored phenomena by logical extrapolation from known phenomena. Given a view of the world, a set of 'facts' which that view has given rise to, and some speculations about how those facts came to be, what *other* states of affairs ought logically to be observable? If the bridge of logical necessity so constructed is a solid one, then the occurrence or non-occurrence of the looked-for state of affairs will have some repercussions – not always straightforward, as we have seen, but some – on the status of the speculations. That is the Popperian method, the 'hypothetico–deductive' one, and it again is part of the scientists' armamentarium, but not the whole of it. It paints scientific progress, if we take it as *the* method of science, as a far more completely rational process than we know it to be. Nevertheless the strength of the reasoning that connects predictions to theories *is* an important part of the quality of scientific work, and criticism of this logic is a familiar part of the routine development of science.

Scientific thinking often differs from its everyday equivalent in being *reflective*. Experiments are not designed in the heat of the moment, in response to an immediate need or frustration. The process of seeing where one's conjectures lead, and contriving new events to observe, may take months of patient planning, thinking and preparation. Scientists have the leisure (ideally, at any rate) to devote a large amount of off-line, deliberate thinking to the business of testing ideas. Much effort goes into making as sure as possible that studies are well-designed – that is, that the data which they throw up, whatever they may be, will be as interesting, as interpretable, as unambiguous, and as germane to the ideas that gave rise to them, as possible. Science relies not just on thinking *about* ideas, but thinking them *through*.

*Generating*

The third of the scientists' core skills is the ability to come up with the ideas that conscious, deliberate, rational thought can then get to work on, refine, and explore for predictions. Here we meet the question, which has often been muddled up with the preceding one, of scientific *creativity*: where do scientific conjectures and speculations come from in the first place. Though the appraisal of theories is at least potentially (though in practice only partly) a matter of rational analysis, the generation of theories is clearly not. They arise in people's minds in the form of hunches, intuitions, blinding insights (which may in the morning turn out to be of less value than they had seemed at 3 a.m.), vague feelings and images, which then have to be *turned* into more logical form if they are not to be forgotten. Albert Einstein himself, the paragon of a scientist, wrote of his own creative process that:

> The words or the language as they are written or spoken do not seem to play any role in my mechanism of thought. The physical entities which seem to serve as elements of thought are certain signs and more or less clear images which can be voluntarily reproduced and combined. . .this combinatory play seems to be the essential feature in productive thought, before there is any connection with logical construction in words or other kinds of sign which can be communicated to others. . .In a stage where words intervene at all, they are, in my case, purely auditive, but they interfere only in a secondary stage.[8]

Such flashes may be stimulated by tiredness, meditation, a joke, a chance association of ideas, or even by a train of thought that purports to be rational but is actually illogical or based on false or even idiotic premises. As Max Charlesworth has written:

> when we look at the actual way in which scientists – from Galileo onwards – have gone on, we see that they are prepared to use any and every method; they rely on intuitions and mystical ideas, they play their hunches, they invent *ad hoc* hypotheses, they resort to bluff and propaganda, they concoct myths and tell fairy stories.[9]

When scientists resort to underhand means to influence the testing of ideas – when they pervert the course of scientific justice – they deserve to be spotted and are rightly censured. But where their ideas come from, short of outright plagiarism, is nobody's business but their own. What matters about a scientific idea is its robustness, not its family history, and as the notorious 'philosopher of science and entertainer' as he has been called, Paul Feyerabend has persuasively argued, the only valid principle, when it comes to creating scientific theories, is 'anything goes'.[10]

### Phases and species of science

Science consists of a mixture of observation, rational thinking, and creative thinking, interacting with each other in disciplined but not always clearly analysable ways. But the emphasis in the mixture, and the form the interactions take, vary considerably depending on the stage that a scientific inquiry is at, and the intrinsic nature of the field of inquiry itself. It is for this reason that the generic description of 'the scientific method' has to be kept at such a general level.

If one takes the simple view that science can *only* be the collection and distillation of true facts, or the rigorous, cyclical process of conjecturing and refuting, then while the contents of science – its accumulation of certain laws, or its current stockpile of not-yet-discredited speculations – may change, the nature of the activity clearly does not. However, if one admits that science is an intricate mixture of activities of different types, then there is no reason to deny that the composition of this mixture may well vary from topic to topic, or as a topic evolves. Nor need there be any objection to the idea that different cultures may have very different images of what science is, or that the image within a culture may alter radically during certain crucial periods of scientific progress. This is precisely what has been argued, and demonstrated, by another famous philosopher of science, originally a physicist, Thomas Kuhn.[11]

The fact that science cannot be boiled down to a single, well-defined method has sometimes been taken to imply, especially by Paul Feyerabend, that it has no method at all. He claims to have shown that any rule for the conduct of science you care to name has been broken in the pursuit of some fruitful scientific advance by someone somewhere in the history of science. Whether this is so or not, this is a quite different thing from proving that there are no *usual* or *common* approaches to scientific discovery.

During the early stages of the investigation of a new problem, scientists  will often make an effort to look in as 'neutral' a way as possible, to try to prevent their preconceptions from channelling their observations and their thoughts, and to 'let the data speak for themselves'. We might call this the 'fishing' stage: one has a hunch that there may be interesting things lurking in a general vicinity, but no clear idea about what they are, or where they might lead. In this mode, scientists come as near as they ever do to operating in the Baconian fashion, as they let the processes of observation, and the *generation* of ideas, run along rather freely, side by side, without much critical commentary from the evaluative quarter. Often this stage involves less deliberate, and more contemplative, types of thinking, as the things that are noticed are fed in a rather unsystematic form into the less conscious parts of the mental computer, which tends to print out, as Einstein said, in intuitions, hunches and images, rather than in maths or neat, articulate prose.

Arising from this reflective phase there may be a period of greater activity, which is still not of strictly experimental form – a period that scientists themselves often refer to as 'messing about', in which various hunches are tried out in a preliminary way, 'to see if they lead anywhere', or simple kinds of probe are applied 'to see what happens'. Lab notebooks may be filled with jottings, many of which are destined never to see the light of day. One 'reads around the subject', and spends intense and highly productive three-hour coffee breaks, locked in discussion, from which one emerges in more of a fog than ever. One is casting around, like a hound looking for the scent, sometimes setting off down several trails and then backtracking, before committing oneself to a particular line of inquiry.

Then may come a phase of full-blown experimentation, where now analytical, logical thinking is very much to the fore, and one tries to design studies that are as 'watertight' as possible by pre-empting all possible criticism, and by meticulous attention to methodological detail. One attempts to simplify and stylise the phenomena of interest, so that putative variables can be manipulated more directly, and their effects seen more clearly. Here the cycle between generation, observation and testing is much tighter, and new ideas tend to emerge as required modifications of existing models, rather than via large leaps of imagination. A programme of research is not a collection of single experimental shots, but an evolving, interdependent set of studies, each of which arises out of reflection on its predecessors. So although science searches for generality, and tries to apply existing principles to new cases, they usually need to be cut to fit, as the data emerge, and cannot just be applied off the peg.

There are intrinsic differences between fields of scientific inquiry in the mix of methods they employ. In physics and chemistry, the well-controlled experiment, product of a logical rationale that issues from a twig-tip of a vast, monolithic tree of accepted theory, and involving expensive machines and complicated sums, is the norm. And it is this that is often held up, in science education, as the be-all and end-all, the epitome, of scientific method. But such a procedure, whilst very powerful, is only possible, and appropriate, with certain subject matter. In palaeontology, the study of the fossil record, or in astronomy, one sometimes cannot contrive the tests one might wish; one cannot interfere with these aspects of nature to see what happens. All one can do – and this, as we see, is still very productive – is to use theories and ideas to *direct one's attention* towards certain kinds and locations of events; and to *guide one's interpretation* of what one sees; while in ethology, the study of animals in their natural environments, one *could* intervene, but by doing so would introduce a perturbation that might lead to results that do not reflect at all the uninterrupted behaviour of the creatures one is watching. It is no use setting up a ring of arc lights in the hope of seeing one's badger more clearly, if one's intention is to see what it does in the dark.

*Routine vs frontier science*
Let me emphasise the variability of science by contrasting two 'versions', similar to those that Thomas Kuhn referred to as 'normal' and 'revolutionary' science, which I shall call 'routine science' and 'frontier science'. In routine science, the tree of scientific knowledge is broad and stable. There is a strong root system of ideas and practices that is taken for granted, and which directs the course of scientific endeavour in a powerful and largely tacit fashion. Though there is still much scope for scientific creativity, it concerns matters of detail: how to settle this local dispute, or how to solve that technical problem. There is not much respect for creativity on the grand scale: people who try to challenge the 'status quo' are more likely to gain disdain than respect – unless they have first demonstrated over many years their ability to contribute to scientific progress *within* the accepted 'paradigm', as Kuhn calls it. Even then, if they overstep the mark too far or for too long, they are likely to be written off with a sad shake of the head, as having 'gone mystical' or lost their grip. In routine science the premium is on work that is technically precise and logically tight, and which serves to dot i's and cross t's: 'mopping up', Kuhn rather disparagingly calls it.

In frontier science, on the other hand, there is much more scope for the free play of ideas. The tree has a much thinner trunk, if we are talking about a new scientific domain; or a much less rigid root system, if we are looking at an established science going through a period of upheaval. Much more is up-for-grabs, in the sense that a greater proportion of the ideas that are around form the subject matter of open discussion, rather than the closed context of presupposition within which discussion takes place. In frontier science, it is likely that much more of the work will consist precisely in unearthing and shaking loose the roots of the established order. Frontier science happens at the base of the trunk, when the rules of thought and of empirical practice which had held tacit sway over the conduct of the subject are now themselves becoming the objects of scrutiny. If the danger in routine science is of nitpicking, the exercise of precision without creativity, the complementary danger of frontier science is handwaving, the unbridled exercise of creativity without the restraining influence of hardheaded testing and analysis.

## The personal context

Theories tend to fade out of the scientific limelight for a number of reasons. They may have suffered a fatal accumulation of critical pinpricks, and have had to be patched up with so many ancillary assumptions and instances of special pleading that they have become increasingly cumbersome or implausible. Or a shift in the underlying framework of assumptions has happened, which renders the theory incompatible with current thinking, and shunts it and its proponents into a siding. Or a persuasive proponent of a new approach appears on the scene. Or (according to 'Plank's dictum') its proponents just pass away or, for any of a host of reasons, lose interest. Most commonly radical change comes about for a combination of these reasons.[12]

What this reminds us of is the fact that scientific theories, as well as resting on a great heap of partially buried assumptions, are also the creatures of flesh and blood human beings, who often have a personal investment in keeping their ideas live, and trying to convert the world to their way of thinking. Thus far from being passive Popperians, for example, most scientists will react to a threatened refutation of their pet theory not by instant capitulation, but by a detailed search for some technical flaw, or 'procedural difference' that will allow them to discount it; or by an attempt to ignore it. Such inertia is not just a reflection of an egotistical reluctance to 'face the facts': in such a complex situation it makes good, rational sense to look for all the possible *alternative* (and quite possibly trivial or boring) explanations for an experimental result, before finally accepting it as a true invalidation of an interesting conjecture.

Thus the process of scientific evolution cannot be fully understood without taking into account the personalities of the scientists themselves. Whether a theory, or a new line of inquiry, becomes established and accepted depends on the quality of research on which it rests, but it also depends on how forcefully and skilfully it is promoted. If the scientists behind it are not knowledgeable, logical and careful, their work will be full of holes: these qualities are necessary, but they are not sufficient. In addition, it helps to be stubborn, energetic, articulate, and well-connected. Let me go into this in a little more detail, using the distinction between routine and frontier science.

What does it take to be a good *routine* scientist? One needs to have mastered the accepted body of information and the range of accepted techniques, that form the trunk of the tree. One needs to be able to talk the language: to raise pertinent questions about experimental method, to confront results or conjectures with inconvenient alternatives, to be adept at suggesting other explanations for putative findings than the one proffered. Much of routine science is of this critical kind; detecting flaws or ambiguities in the existing literature, and exposing them to well-conceived empirical test, or tightly-argued rebuttal. The link between the subject-matter of the domain and the kinds of questions and arguments that carry weight is close; you cannot be an effective routine scientist without both knowing what there is to be known, *and* being able to analyse and test that knowledge effectively. You do not need to understand what the roots are of the tree you are busy pruning, or even to be aware of them. The papers you submit are within the parameters that these tacit presuppositions have established, and therefore they are likely to be judged by the rational criteria which those assumptions dictate. Knowledgeability and attention to detail are what will get you through – being able to spot little holes and to plug them soundly.

Frontier scientists also need to be able to 'think straight': to design watertight experiments and to argue convincingly, if they are to be forces to be reckoned with. But they differ from their more routine colleagues in needing to be able to think in terms of larger patterns, and particularly to be aware of the assumptions that others are taking for granted. Only when a belief is changed in status from a presupposition to a questionable contention can alternatives be considered, and the particular bent of the frontier scientist, therefore, is to investigate the known, rather than the unknown. For this, much greater independence of mind, persistence in the face of lack of interest and absence of encouragement, tolerance for uncertainty, and a penchant for quiet reflection as well as busy activity, are the requisite characteristics. Posing a bigger challenge to the workaday habits of the scientific establishment, the frontier scientist must be prepared for a greater amount of *ad hominem* scrutiny, and seemingly irrational responses. The more tightly held the framework that is being criticised, the stronger will the resistance be. Conversely in times of self-doubt, when respected members of the community are publicly expressing dissatisfaction with the status quo, or in subjects that have not yet evolved a guiding mythology, then there is much more scope and tolerance for the more creative thinkers. There is more of a chance that they will be perceived as saviours rather than as heretics.[13]

### The social world of science.

Not only is the scientific enterprise subject to such irrational, individual factors as the scientists' temperaments, ambitions or the competing priorities and attractions in their lives; it also depends on judgements that are made by the scientific sub-culture. The naive idea that 'scientific knowledge' accumulates as the result of irrefutable demonstrations – that the *only* thing that matters in swaying the community is the logical and technical precision of one's experiments – has also to be supplemented, if we are to tell the story as it is, rather than as we might like it to be, with a host of less rational social forces. For example, whether the ploy of trying to ignore or explain away hostile results is successful or not will depend on how much the rest of the scientific community is interested in the dispute, and the relative esteem in which they hold you and your antagonist.

The recent sociology of science is full of examples of the way what has come to count as 'scientific knowledge' has been influenced by this powerful social network, acting both formally and informally.[14] Formally senior colleagues, journal referees, publishers' academic consultants, appointing committees and examiners exercise quality control over what gets published and who gets promoted. The editor of a perfectly respectable journal, *Environmental Ethics*, for example, was persistently refused tenure by the philosophy department of the University of Georgia where he worked on the grounds that his editorship did not, in the majority view, 'count as significant scholarly and professional activity', and that *none* of his substantial number of publications in the area of environmental ethics – which deals with conceptual and theoretical issues in the science of ecology – was of sufficient quality to meet the standards of the department.[15] The publications may or may not have been brilliant, but their intrinsic merit is not at stake. What we are seeing here is the academic community making a judgement about the validity of a novel field of scientific inquiry, a judgement that is currently (1991) in the process of being challenged worldwide.

Informally the network of those who have already gained respect within a scientific community exchanges notes about who and what to watch out for, both positively and negatively, over coffee at conferences and in postscripts to more official letters. Whether an unusual result, or a provocative article, gets published, may depend as much on a breakdown in the process of blind reviewing, which allows information about the authors and their pedigrees to influence the decision process, as on the apparent technical merit of the work submitted.

The more unlikely the result, or the more a conjecture challenges taken-for-granted assumptions at the root of the tree, the more such factors may play a part. Although the scientific community officially checks claims by trying to replicate them, in practice attempts at exact replication are surprisingly rare (and perfect replication is of course a logical impossibility).[16] It is more usual for any consequent experiment to vary the conditions, even if only slightly; but this of course leaves it open for the original team or individual to claim that a failure to replicate is due not to any fault in their procedure, but to the introduction of these 'procedural variations'. So doubts about the validity of a result are hard to settle empirically. Instead judgements about whether to 'accept' it or not (i.e. whether to publish it, and/or to take any notice of it) are influenced strongly by an emerging consensus on the part of the 'elders' in the area, about whether the experiment was competently conducted or not. What is on trial, in the informal court, is not the result *per se*, but the experimenter.

This social moderation of what is to count as scientific knowledge, or acceptable procedure, has its good and its bad sides, of course. When the elders are benign, their experience provides a valuable source of quality control. They are able to spot promising young scientists and offer them useful patronage. But when either their scientific or social attitudes are too entrenched, then the same system can act to undermine theoretical opponents, hold back threateningly bright juniors, and perpetuate prejudice and privilege.

## The social/political context

The final skin of the onion, its outermost layer, concerns the forces that impinge on science from external, non-scientific sources. Topics are taken up or dropped as a result of changing fashions in social attitudes. Life is made uncomfortable for those scientists who experiment on live animals, or attempt to make racially-based comparisons of IQ. Alternatively money suddenly becomes available for the testing of AIDS-related drugs, or for the development of environment-friendly aerosols and washing powders. As governments change, so differing priorities for research are set; different mechanisms for funding are introduced; cash limits are imposed or relaxed; universities are starved or fattened. Scientists, like everyone else, work in a world of fluctuating opportunities and constraints, and the quality and direction of research will be influenced by these, and by the way they are perceived. Currently huge amounts of money are available for research on AIDS and cancer, or on the science behind certain weapon systems, for example, while so-called pure research is being cut back across the board. Pharmaceutical companies wave fat cheques under the noses of academic pharmacologists, which, if accepted, are bound to bring with them pressures on the drugs to be tested, and the results that are sought.

## SCIENCE PROPER: A SUMMARY

I shall leave the major consideration of the implication of this discussion for science education until Chapters 6 and 7, when we consider what image of science it is desirable for young people to leave school with. Let me here just highlight some of the points that I shall be picking up then. Science is very hard to define clearly. At its centre is the attempt to generate comprehensive accounts of phenomena in the natural world which give rise to accurate predictions, and therefore to the possibility of greater control, within particular domains. This attempt is embedded, however, within a context of personal psychology and social influence, which renders it fallible and slow. Scientific 'knowledge' is actually an intricate body of relatively successful ideas, and could therefore not get oV the ground without human faculties that are non-logical, intuitive and reflective. To misquote Polonius, 'though this be method, yet there's madness in't'.

But equally the faculty of 'straight thinking' is needed, in order to devise ways of telling the successful from the unsuccessful ideas. 'Creativity' throws up candidate hypotheses; 'rational problem solving' and 'hypothe-tico-deductive thinking' sort the wheat from the chaff. This recursive act of threshing leaves behind it an untidy pile of 'unconscious presuppositions', 'self-evident truths', 'disputed facts' and 'bold conjectures', and lets the wind carry away the disproved claims and the misconceptions. At each stage in the development of scientific ideas, what is 'obvious' today was 'ridiculous' yesterday and will be 'false' tomorrow.

Science education has the option of focusing on many aspects, and mixtures of aspects, of this story. At present it tends to teach theories as if they were incontrovertible, offering in compensation perhaps a few historical vignettes that do little to dispel that impression. The role of idea-generation, and the evolutionary nature of science are not stressed; and the influence of non-rational personal and social factors is not discussed. Differences between the methods of different sciences are hardly pointed out, and little is done to question lay mythology about either the power or the dangers of science. There is only scant chance to practise the special skills of 'fishing' and 'messing about', and not enough responsibility provided to sharpen up reflection-in-action.[17]

## NOTES

[1] Robin Millar, (ed.) *Doing Science: Images of science in science education*, Falmer: London, 1989.

[2] A.F. Chalmers, *What is this Thing Called Science?*, University of Queensland Press, 1976; 2nd edition, Open University Press: Milton Keynes, 1982.

[3] Werner Heisenberg, *Physics and Philosophy*, Allen and Unwin: London, 1963.

[4] From Millar, *op. cit.*

[5] Karl Popper, *Conjectures and Refutations*, Routledge and Kegan Paul: London, 1969.

[6] I. Lakatos and A. Musgrave, *Criticism and the Growth of Knowledge*, CUP: Cambridge, 1970.

[7] See Richard Bergland, *The Fabric of the Mind*, Penguin: Ringwood, Victoria, Australia, 1985.

[8] Albert Einstein, *Ideas and Opinions*, Souvenir Press: London, 1973.

[9] Max Charlesworth, *Science, Non-Science and Pseudo-Science*, Deakin University Press, 1982.

[10] Paul Feyerabend, *Against Method*, New Left Books: London, 1975.

[11] Thomas Kuhn, *The Structure of Scientific Revolutions*, University of Chicago Press: Chicago, 1970.

[12] *ibid.*

[13] Though large-scale innovators invariably receive something of a rough ride – witness the attacks of people like Richard Dawkins in *The Extended Phenotype*, W.H. Freeman: Oxford, 1982, on the Gaia hypothesis, a perfectly respectable and testable scientific proposal by James Lovelock in his *Gaia: A New Look at Life on Earth*, OUP: Oxford, 1979.

[14] See Harry Collins, *Changing Order:Replication and Induction in Scientific Practice*, Sage: London, 1985; G. Holton, *The Scientific Investigation*, CUP: Cambridge, 1978; and B. Latour and S. Woolgar, *Laboratory Life: The Social Construction of Scientific Facts*, Sage: Beverley Hills, 1979.

[15] This case is considered by Warwick Fox in *Toward a Transpersonal Ecology*, Shambhala: Boston, 1990.

[16] See Collins, *op. cit.*

[17] Good general discussions of the philosophy of science are provided by A. F. Chalmers, *op. cit.*; *Max Charlesworth, op. cit.*; and Peter Medewar, *Advice to a Young Scientist*, Harper and Row: London, 1979. For good discussions of the way social judgement influences the validation of scientific knowledge, see G. Holton (ed.), *The Scientific Investigation,* CUP: Cambridge, 1978; Latour and Woolgar, *op. cit.*; and Collins, *op. cit.*. For several views on the implicit philosophy of science permeating science education, see Millar *op. cit.*

# CHAPTER FIVE

———— . ————

# THE STUDENT AS SCIENTIST

And suppose we solve all the problems it presents. What happens? We end up with more problems than we started with. Because that's the way problems propagate their species. A problem left to itself dries up or goes rotten. But fertilise a problem with a solution – you'll hatch out dozens.

N.F. Simpson

So far we have looked at two of the slogans of contemporary science education: 'real-life problem solving' and 'the processes of real science'. In both cases we have revealed considerable depths of complexity below these appealing phrases, and have discovered that they are by no means as easy to act upon as they are to say. The intent to enhance everyday competence is bedevilled by the huge problems involved in trying to teach people skills in one situation that you want them to be able to use in very different situations. The aim of giving students an induction into the world of 'science proper' becomes much less clear-cut once we go beyond the simplistic caricature of science as a purely individual and rational encounter between Nature and a human being. Now I want to turn to the third of the grand types of claim that are around at the moment: the idea that science education can help young people develop their abilities as learners. This is an even more sweeping ambition than the 'real-life problem solving' one. There we at least had some grasp of what it was we were hoping to improve, and the majority of difficulties that we revealed were practical ones. When we are trying to help young people 'learn how to learn', however, there really is very little intuitive sense, let alone explicit consensus, about what this means.[1] How *do* people learn? Of what does 'learning ability' consist? Can it really be improved, whatever it is? What conditions are most conducive to its development?

Only recently has psychology become sophisticated enough – or brave enough – to be able to try to build models of learning that bear any relationship to the realities of human beings.[2] Previous theories that were borrowed from the animal world, or which were aimed at accounting for the way in which undergraduates remembered lists of words, could never exercise much appeal for schoolteachers. They were too remote to help them get a purchase on the intricate, shifting world of real students learning in real classrooms. Without models that enabled us to say what we meant by 'learning', and 'learning to learn', we were unable to get beyond general nostrums based more on sentiment than science.

## THE LEARNER AS SCIENTIST

One view that has held out some promise especially to science educators is that developed from the pioneering ideas of George Kelly.[3] Whereas educators had been wondering how to help learners *become* scientists, Kelly suggested that they already, in some sense, *are* scientists. Scientists are people who have ideas about how the world works, and which way it will jump if you prod it; and who like to test those ideas against reality by devising experiments and collecting data. Just so, people at large also live their lives on the basis of a vast collection of theories, beliefs and understandings which they have picked up from experience or tuition, and which they are in the everyday business of acting on, assessing and refining. Even though they are less systematic perhaps, or less explicit about their ideas and experiments, nevertheless they can be seen as informal counterparts of the people who make their living from science proper. The metaphor of the 'learner-as-scientist' has been widely taken up by the literature of science education recently.[4] The idea of science lessons as being for the development of the 'process skills' of science seems to be given psychological support by viewing the student as being a 'natural' scientist.

Now metaphors are helpful to the extent that the image they use is intuitively clear and accessible. The metaphor of water flowing through pipes, for the flow of current in an electrical circuit, is useful only if the students already know, and are in tacit agreement, about water, pipes, and the behaviour of one in the other. And the metaphor of learner-as-scientist works to help form a picture of the learner if we already have a picture of the scientist. However, as we have seen in the last chapter, the image of scientists as people rationally engaged in testing and modifying theories on the basis of experiments, offers only the most crude, and in some ways an inaccurate, picture. We have identified many more ingredients than this in the scientific process; and we have seen that to be a scientist may mean very different things, depending on the state of the science, and the bent of the person.

A metaphor that is general, vague or incomplete can take us only so far. In order to use it to give us any more leverage on the nature of learning, or to see where it may be misleading, it is necessary to feed into it a more sophisticated set of ideas about science. We have to ask: 'What kind of scientists are science students supposed to be?' Are they more like routine or frontier scientists? Do they behave like the logical automata of scientific mythology, or like the fallible, self-interested, socially-sensitive, flesh-and-blood people whom one finds in real labs? What sorts of theories do they hold? How are these theories organised? Are there any intrinsic patterns to their development? What kinds of attitudes and abilities do the junior 'scientists' possess? Do these vary from age to age, and if so how? Where do they get their ideas from? What influence on the development of their personal theories is exerted by the societies and cultures to which they belong? Do they have any choice or leeway concerning the kind of 'scientist' they are going to be? When we have explored these questions, we will then be able to ask: what kinds of learners – and what kinds of scientists, both literal and metaphorical – should we be aiming to produce?

## CONSTRUCTIVISM

The guiding image of the learner-as-scientist rests on the idea that people at large are no more passive receivers of information than scientists-proper are; their 'experiments' and interpretations have to be seen as reflecting theories and hypotheses actively constructed by people out of their experience, and actively involved in attempting to make sense out of the constant stream of new situations in which they find themselves. All psychological functions – perceiving and acting, as well as learning – operate in terms of people's past experiences, and the residue that those experiences has left.[5] You cannot see, or feel, or imagine, or remember, or know, except by using what you *already* know. Past experience is not only accumulated in terms of *what* we know; more importantly it becomes dissolved in *the way* we know – the processes whereby we construe the past, present and future. However dry or regimented a learning experience may be, for example, the learner must always be understood as being in the business of making personal sense of the situation, and not simply as absorbing impressions or 'facts' like a sponge.

How people deal with each moment is a reflection of both the past and the present. It reflects the past, in that previous experience has equipped them with a repertoire of capabilities and dispositions, anxieties and interests, knowledge and expectations. It is a function of the present in that the current setting will activate certain of those attitudes and abilities, and not others; and depending on how learners are readied, so their construction of, and their reaction to, the situation will be different. To put it simply, if you have previously been treated unfairly or unkindly by your science teacher, you may well have been left with a residue of fear and resentment. Thus as you enter the science laboratory *now*, you are tacitly 'setting yourself', like an electronic burglar alarm, to react in certain ways to what happens – not to try, to believe you are stupid, to withdraw into yourself, to think spiteful thoughts about the teacher, and so on. Or alternatively if you have just finished reading *The Selfish Gene*, the difficult bits of which were well explained to you by your elder sister, who is in the third year of a biology degree, then you are readied to be bored by your teacher's laboured and simplistic introduction to evolutionary genetics, and to amuse yourself by asking increasingly crass questions, to see at what point the teacher twigs that nobody, not even you, could be so stupid.

The learner-as-scientist point of view strongly suggests that students can be expected to arrive at science lessons with some pre-existing notions about scientific phenomena, and to try to make sense of the lesson topics in terms of those beliefs and expectations. And the attribution to learners of such 'theories' seems, as I say, to tie the metaphor together in a satisfying way. Thus, as we saw in Chapter 1, many researchers around the world have gone off to classrooms to look for evidence of these 'implicit theories', or 'alternative conceptions', as they are sometimes called.[6] Sure enough they have discovered that young people turn out to hold many quaint beliefs about the world which are at odds with the scientifically respected ones. Many believe that 'weeds are not plants' – because 'plants' have to be cultivated. Nor are trees – they are too big to be 'plants'. Steam turns into air when you can no longer see it. Light travels further at night. Electric current gets used up in light bulbs. For things to move there has to be a force on them. Aluminium foil will keep a block of ice cream frozen for longer than a blanket will. Cold water freezes faster than hot water. It is just as well that we are on the top of the world, or the force of gravity would pull us off. And so on. (Adult readers too may well find themselves in tacit agreement with at least some of these unscientific beliefs.)[7]

It is clearly of interest to know that young people do have such ideas: teachers can make allowances for the fact that they are not starting from scratch, sowing science into virgin mental soil, so to speak, but are having to engage with a tangled undergrowth of pre-existing beliefs. Students' difficulties with the concepts of formal science may be due less to the fact that the new ideas are 'falling on stony ground' than that they are being 'choked by thorns'. This realisation has led many researchers to advise that time devoted to exploring the brushwood, before introducing the new seedlings, would be time well spent. Being good constructivists, they know that they cannot climb inside children's heads and do the gardening for them; they have to encourage them to want to exchange the old ideas for the new ones, by seeing for themselves that the new ones work better.

However there is so far little evidence that teaching approaches based on encouraging individual reflection, small-group sharing of intuitions, and deliberately engineering conflict between new and old ideas (which of course reveals the superiority of the new) produce better learning. This may at least partly be due to the fact that constructivism puts so much more into the pedagogical melting-pot than just the implicit theories students hold about the contents of lessons. Once you admit learners' ideas, you also have to acknowledge the actual or potential importance of their interests, fears, self-image, ambitions and resources. And you have to be aware of the many aspects of the current scene – especially its social aspects – that are going to be plucking these strings in particular sequences and combinations. It is a racing certainty that these factors will turn out to account for a much greater proportion of the variance in students' performance in science than either their funny ideas or their so-called 'ability'.[8] Espousing constructivism, and using it only to validate an interest in students' scientific intuitions, is like getting yourself a tiger to catch mice. It is far too big and powerful for the job, and you are likely to find it getting out of hand.

## MINITHEORIES

Concern with young people's own knowledge arose as an attempt to counteract the traditional emphasis in science education on facts and ideas that were largely remote from their own personal experience. The other response to this preponderance of factual learning has been, as we have discussed already, to concentrate on the *processes* of science. While one can sympathise with those who wished to free school science from the deadening influence of a concept-dominated curriculum in this way, their assumptions about the separability of know-how from know-that were naive. Psychology is not on their side, for it turns out that it is the norm in mental organisation for knowledge and skill to be stored together, in purpose-built packages, which have evolved to meet the range of demands which can be expected in a particular type of familiar situation or 'scenario'.[9] This combination of content, context, purpose and process into flexible bundles of localised competence is the primary format of the mind. Far from being the neat, coherent unitary sort of theory to which science proper aspires, the mind-scape of the child is patchwork and piecemeal. It consists not of a single integrated theory but of an assembly of 'minitheories', each generated to provide successful engagement with a particular kind of scenario.

These modules of understanding are built up on the basis of accumulated experience within that scenario, and they act rather like different disks, or files, on a computer. Every change of context or priorities may act to select a new 'file', and this then sets the person's sensitivities and capabilities. What they see and how they respond will vary, depending on what file happens to be running. It is also the currently active file which is the one that will be modified by any learning that takes place. Files are 'indexed' according to the type of situation they have been found to be useful in. Thus their 'labels' can be a mixture of perceptual features and motivational states. There may be different files for the same situation or 'topic', each organised round a different kind of purpose that a person might have.

For example, though we might designate 'sex' as a single topic or concept, a typical male adolescent may have several quite distinct mini-theories for dealing with sexual matters, depending on the purpose and the context he finds himself in. In biology lessons, sex means the process of conception, the transmission of AIDS, and some long latin-y words. It means trying to look serious and feeling slightly embarrassed. In his gang of male friends, sex means showing off, dirty jokes and crude language. In private, sex may mean Adrian Mole-ish anxieties, grandiose fantasies and the guilty pleasure of masturbation. With his first girl-friend, sex means the awful anxieties about how far and how fast to go, and furtive attempts to engineer touch in the guise of horse-play, massage or comfort. There may be almost no overlay between the contents of these four minitheories. The idea of telling dirty jokes to a girl-friend may seem abhorrent; and information about contraception mysteriously fails to come to mind at exactly the moment when it is needed.

In another corner of the same person's mind we might find the same type of dissociation with respect to quite a different topic. Information about 'relative velocity' is filed under 'Physics', not under 'Trains', so that when casually dropping stones off a railway bridge into the path of an express, he simply has no awareness that what he is doing is equivalent to throwing the stone at the windscreen of a stationary train at 100 miles per hour. In a sense he *has* the relevant information, but it does not come to mind, and so does not influence his actions.

### EARLY LEARNING

It might help to clarify this idea of 'patchwork cognition' if I give a brief sketch of how it gets started, and how it develops.[10] The young baby's first minitheories develop around its precious interactions with its mother: it learns over the first few months of life to piece together a multi-media 'image' of the way she looks, smells, feels, tastes and sounds; of the kinds of rituals that she habitually tries to involve the baby in; and most important-ly of all, of the ways in which her responses are contingent, even if only subtly, on the part the baby itself takes in these interactions. One of the first minitheories, for example, evolves around the vital episodes of feeding, and the baby rapidly learns the 'script', the part it is expected to play if all is to go smoothly and the quality of the service is to remain high. As developmental psychologists have recently argued, if the baby's top priority is to get its biological needs met, it very quickly learns to translate that quest into the search for engagement in, or 'attunement with', its immediate social world.[11] Dependent upon others for help, it soon discovers that its best bet is to join in the social dance that is going on around it, and to learn the steps as well as it can.

This continues to be the case as the child begins to differentiate its primordial minitheories into others that correspond to the increasing range of social events in which it takes part – nappy-changing, bath-time, playing peek-a-boo, arrivals and departures of other people, and so on. The child begins to develop a repertoire of social scripts, and of the parts that it can happily play within each. So the first kind of learning that causes the mind-scape to expand is the *splitting* and *refining* of earlier minitheories to meet the needs more exactly of a widening variety of encounters. In the classic example, the six-month-old shows no fear of strangers, and relates to them in more or less the same way as it would to its close family. Very soon, however, many babies show a marked difference of behaviour when introduced to a new person. They do not automatically try to engage the stranger in their familiar scripts, but act much more circumspectly, having discovered that 'new' people may wish to write with the baby an original playlet for them to act out jointly, and are unwilling or unable simply to step in and understudy an existing role.

The next kind of learning, so smoothly embarked upon that it is tempting to see it as innate, is to *experiment* with the rituals; to try out some ad-libs, and see whether the social harmony is enhanced, sustained or ruptured by so doing. This experimentation only occurs within the confident framework of a well-understood script, so that, if an ad-lib falls flat, there is an easy fall-back into the old familiar ways. But it allows a greater degree of flexibility to be introduced into the script, which has the benefit of generating more fun, and expanding the child's learning. The fundamental stock of skill that a minitheory contains slowly proliferates into a framework for operating, plus a whole range of options and 'contingency plans'. Thus children come to be able not just to take part in stereotyped rituals, but to improvise within the basic stage directions that have been laid down.

Minitheories evolve both in their internal complexity, and in their 'location' – the domain of experiences which they have been found to handle. As well as promoting development in the content of their expertise, experience is constantly refining the way they are indexed, so that their spheres of influence come to be more and more clearly specified. Sometimes this sort of tuning involves changing an aspect of this specification, so that, for instance, instead of being 'called up' by all cats and small dogs indiscriminately, the same set of responses and attitudes is now activated by cats but not by chihuahuas. But very often, especially during the earlier stages of development, features of the world to which a minitheory is seen as being relevant are not swapped but dropped, so that the expertise which it contains acquires wider utility. This process is the one that has recently come to be called *disembedding*.[12] Learning proceeds by generalising what we already know, as well as by altering it, and we are thus able to capitalise more and more effectively on the skills that we have. Instead of treating all new acquaintances as requiring fresh competence, we are able to discover that some of them may be assimilated easily into habitual patterns of interaction. Others, of course, will not be so conveniently dealt with. As you try to 'dance' with them in your familiar way, they initially keep treading on your toes, and seem to prefer an interpersonal tango to your family's invariable foxtrot. And others may so dislike children that you had better learn to keep off the dance-floor altogether when they are around.

These basic skills of evolutionary learning are often eclipsed by the more eye-catching strategies that develop later, but it is good to remember that they form the bedrock of our learning ability throughout the entire lifespan. They become so well-practised and familiar that we hardly notice them, yet the majority of adult learning, as well as that of the child, is of this sort. Our daily expertise, which we take so much for granted, consists of minitheories that are designed to help us deal smoothly with the situations that we most commonly find ourselves in – family, work, friends, leisure pursuits and so on. From the rituals of family breakfast, to the virtuosity of programming a computer or playing a cello, we are relying upon, and constantly retuning, these packages of competence. Meeting new people, updating or retraining job skills, trying new food, taking holidays in new countries, moving in to a new house. . .all of these require us to tune and modify our existing minitheories, and to split and combine them as we discover additional similarities and differences between the scenarios in which we take part.[13] The body of knowledge in the mind grows and divides into a variegated cellular structure, just as the physical body does.

The first understandings of the physical world that the child gains germinate, so to speak, within a social womb. Children are simultaneously learning about the contingent moods, tolerances and preferences of those around them; and about the patterns to be found in the material world. By dropping something fragile on the floor, you are exploring the breaking point of both your mug and your mother. Infant scientists are very busy

trying to detect patterns in their experience, building new or modified
theories to account for and predict those patterns, and increasingly carrying
out their own experiments to persuade the world to reveal itself in areas
of special interest. But their interest in the physical world – the domains
on which their 'scientific' understandings will be founded – is inextricably
tied to their overriding need to stay social. When the chips are down,
mother is much more important than the teacup; and so the freedom to
find out about how 'stuff' behaves is only present when the social world
is quiet and secure. Children are psychologists and sociologists before they
are biologists and physicists; and the pre-eminence of these social and
emotional priorities will direct the course of their learning for many years.[14]

So children at this stage are 'scientists' of a sort. They hold theories about
the world with differing degrees of confidence, and are busy modifying
them in the light of fresh data. They are even initiating their own
'experiments' in order to generate data that will be particularly relevant to
a current area of theoretical interest or weakness.[15] They are inquisitive,
but they are impulsive and inexpert scientists. Their experiments are public
and risky, often clumsily performed and resulting in distress or panic. And
the experiments are perpetually likely to be disrupted by the emergence
of a more pressing biological or social need. Scientists proper do not
routinely abandon their experiments at crucial stages just because they feel
a pang of homesickness. Infants typically do.

Their guesses and hypotheses are uneducated. If their learning efforts
fail, they have nothing else to fall back on. They are unable to raise their
game. When the world becomes out-of-the-ordinary, they are helpless
and dependent, totally reliant on external guidance and protection. And
though they are good with minor variations, they lack knowledge or
insight into the implicit assumptions on which their world rests, and so are
committed to trying to track it, regardless of where it leads. So if their
family dance is a weird or perverted one, for example, all they can do is
keep trying to master it. They cannot question it.

## STRATEGIC LEARNING

These evolutionary forms of learning are essential to get the development
of the mental landscape started, and continue to subserve the process of
fine-tuning that life demands. But they are slow and small-scale. They can
only cope with events that fall on the margins of what is already known;
anything more remote or challenging than that has simply to be avoided
or ignored. And this capacity to shrug off what you cannot yet handle is a
useful one, provided there are caretakers about who will shield you from
*real* danger when it crops up. Contrary to the belief of some early childhood

educators, babies are not overwhelmed by what they cannot yet grasp, and do not have to be protected from complexity that they are not ready to understand.[16] They simply leave it till later.

Nevertheless, young children are constrained, in the learning stakes, by their inability to do more than tinker. Their only strategy for finding out what 'works', when an old script fails to deliver the expected outcome, is to create minor modifications of what they had been doing before, try them out, and see what happens. Do it harder, louder, longer, higher, slower, tighter, or with a bit more vibrato.[17] Trial and error is a weak strategy for two reasons: it does not incorporate a way of producing *good* guesses about what might do; and the 'error' part of the process is overt, so you constantly run the risk of making matters worse before you hit on the way to make them better. If you try to get attention by crying louder, when your parents are trying to ignore you and get a brief bit of peace and quiet, you may end up with more attention than you bargained for.

Luckily other, more powerful forms of learning are capable of being generated by this evolutionary process itself. As well as allowing us to become more expert with predicaments that are familiar, it begins to detect ways of operating that can help us when things are more unsure. We start to learn to learn more skilfully. One very important type of learning involves the gradual disembedding of particularly useful skills and operations from the details of the minitheories within which they were first discovered and developed. Contrary to the idea that mental skills – and especially *learning* skills – just naturally float around in some general-purpose way inside the head, waiting to be called up by any situation to which they are potentially relevant, their expanding sphere of applicability has to be revealed, in an evolutionary fashion, by a gradual erosion of the incidental details of the scenarios within which they were learnt. And this process of disembedding is never absolute; however general a skill or learning strategy has become, it will always retain some specification of the situations in which, and the purposes for which, it is believed to be good. Mental skills are like the core of a gobstopper: experience has to dissolve away their contextual coating before the breadth of their usefulness can be revealed. As we shall see, it is ignorance of this gradual and evolutionary nature of cognitive skill acquisition that has created the mixture of frustration and ineffectiveness with which education, especially science education, has for many students been associated.

As children are growing little 'pods' of mental and physical skill within the germinators of their familiar social scripts, so they are also beginning to discover that these pods have functions and utilities beyond their original purposes and contexts. Through their experimenting, the pods are not only expanding but some of them are becoming disembedded. The skill of imitation, originally used within a game-playing context to create warm, well-attuned exchanges with an older person, is revealed, opportunistically, to hold potential as a learning strategy. As well as causing laughter, experiments reveal that I can sometimes solve a problem of my own by trying to imitate the actions of somebody else. Now, given this new, crude but potentially very powerful hypothesis, I can set about exploring its scope, limitations and variations. A range of abilities, raised within the social nursery, can be capitalised upon in the search for more potent learning strategies, and once the initial hunch has been formed, they can be refined and sharpened in just the same way that other abilities are. Except that now their 'location' or 'address' in the landscape of experience is not 'playing peek-a-boo with Dad' but 'searching for a clue about how to resolve a frustration'.

Learning strategies improve learning power in a number of ways. They can direct us towards better data – more relevant, more rich or more unambiguous with respect to the particular predicament we happen to be facing. They can help us produce better guesses, better hypotheses about what might work in this situation, which we can then try out. They help us make use of 'off-duty' time, when no pressing demand is present, to rehearse our moves, and play useful games of 'what if?' and 'let's see'. And they provide us with ways of exploiting what we already know to greater advantage and in greater safety.[18] Let me just give one illustration – a very important one.

One breakthrough that the young child makes, of great value for the subsequent acceleration of learning, is the discovery of *inner* play: the world of fantasy and imagination. If the first stage of 'impulsive' science corresponds roughly to Piaget's 'sensorimotor period', then the 'imaginative' scientist is 'concrete operational'.[19] Again it is probable that the ability to 'run' a minitheory internally, in order to try out variations and combinations of actions that have not been directly experienced yet, is nurtured socially. Children's fantasies and imaginative extensions of reality, even though they may constitute factual impossibilities, are encouraged. They are 'charming', and though at first the child may not know quite what it was that got the applause, she will soon learn that imagination is fun. But once she is able to control her imagination – it has begun to 'pod' within its parent scripts – she is ripe for the discovery that this same activity can give her educated guesses about how to solve learning problems, and has the benefit of not requiring, until the testing stage, direct exposure to the tangible consequences of getting it wrong. Children become able to see themselves as actors within inner dramas, and thereby to explore actions and roles, events and feelings, that would be too strange or too scary to encounter 'for real'.

This gives an enormous boost to their learning ability, making it at once safer, less impulsive and more creative. Instead of having to act to learn, now children can follow through the possible ramifications of a range of options in their minds, and this gives them the chance of discovering unanticipated benefits of options that did not, at first glance, look the most promising. They might be able to discover, through improvisations on the inner stage, ways of acting that meet more than one need, or which satisfy without antagonising. Between the want and the act intervenes the intuition or the image, and learners are thus equipped with an additional point at which they can appraise a candidate idea about how to cope. Of course a happy ending in fantasy by no means guarantees a similar outcome in reality. But as imagination becomes more disciplined, so it becomes a valuable source of hunches and hypotheses; ones that may be at the same time safer and bolder than those of pure trial and error.

## LANGUAGE AND THOUGHT [20]

When language arrives, children quickly discover the learning potential of chattering and eavesdropping. Originally emerging as the primary cement holding the social world together, language, like imitation and imagination, turns out to bring with it other benefits too. Listening in on others' thoughts and plans gives children, like the rest of us, an invaluable source of data about how those people are likely to react to our interventions, and enables us to time and adjust our actions accordingly. Talking enables us to enlist other people's support with our own learning projects. Just as imitation started out as an interaction with a social purpose, which then revealed itself to have potential as a learning tool, so the child discovers that the rudiments of social chat can be modified slightly to produce 'requests' and 'questions'.[21]

But as well as these 'external' functions, it has been suggested that language has an amazingly liberating effect on the internal organisation of the mind.[22] It enables different minitheories to talk to each other; to call each other up when they are stuck and ask each others' advice. Before language, each module developed relatively independently of the others, this being, up to a point, an efficient way of organising an increasingly complicated set of cognitive tools. When a minitheory was 'running', its theories were being put to the test of experience, and developed accordingly. But if a problem arose that the theory could not be easily modified to deal with, it was stymied. And when that minitheory was not running, any experience that cropped up could have no effect on it, however relevant it might potentially have been.

Put crudely, we might look on the development of language as going through four stages. First, small fragments of speech become embedded within a host of different minitheories. Mealtimes, bathtimes and toilet-times all have recurrent slogans going along with them that the child comes to recognise and respond to. Following a little behind comes her ability to join in the chat with approved gurgles, and then words and short utterances, of her own. Second, still within individual minitheories, dawns the realisation that certain chunks of speech are intended to correspond to certain chunks of the non-verbal scenario – portions of the environment, and segments of the action. The break-up of originally seamless scripts into sub-scripts or 'concepts', the trans-situational constituents, is accelerated by the association of each of the components with a distinctive sound.

Thus, third, it becomes possible to connect elements of different scripts together with the links that are formed to these words. 'Mummy' can be dissected out of her different scenarios and can be treated as an entity, an ingredient of the child's life which can be relied upon to carry with her, from script to script, some constant features and dispositions. So the modular landscape begins to develop in a different direction. As well as being organised by *contexts*, recurrent situations in which the child finds herself, she becomes able to operate also in terms of the concepts that keep cropping up in different places.

Finally the world of words begins to grow its own interconnections. Not only can a word call up ideas and concepts that have been abstracted from a range of separate minitheories; words come to be able to call up each other. Overlaid on the patchwork landscape of minitheories, each of which is unable to talk directly to the others, is a network of connections, the words and syntax of the language, through which they come to be able to communicate. It is as if a flotilla of boats, whose captains had previously been prevented from talking to each other directly, is suddenly equipped with two-way radios. Now when one minitheory is operating, and hits a snag, it can try *describing* the situation, and asking *questions* to which it does not itself have the answer, which is like broadcasting an SOS. Somewhere out on the airwaves another minitheory, not previously active but nevertheless listening in, might radio back with just the piece of information, or the offer of the particular skill, that you need. Or it might say 'Hold on a minute; let me come alongside and we will see if we can put our heads together about it.' Thus with language the mind of the learner becomes able to capitalise on its own accumulated resources in a way that had previously been prevented by the modular structure, and which gives it enormously increased ability to solve its own problems.

As development proceeds, so language reveals more and more of its potential as a learning resource. It permits internal and external communication; but it is also the soil within which reason and logic can take hold, and through the cultivation of these attributes, learning can become enormously more intellectual, deliberate and articulate. Logic enables us to build longer, stronger arms reaching out from what we know into the realms of the unknown. We can subject our ideas and assumptions to more powerful tests if we can say with confidence that *if* such-and-such is true, then a certain state of affairs *must* also be true. It is such mental skills that the scientist proper is going to need in abundance, and which are useful tools for everyone to have at their disposal.

### MINITHEORIES FROM SCRATCH

Language and imagination together open up for learners a very useful new option. Not only are they enabled to construct solutions to learning challenges that are more inventive and more remote from their own first-hand experience; they are able, if it seems appropriate, to set up new minitheories that are not merely outgrowths of existing ones. Through reading and listening, and especially through instruction and tuition, the building-blocks of a new domain of understanding can be assembled. Just as language can conjure up non-existent concepts, like a flying pig, or the cathedral in the middle of the beach, so it can be used to create *de novo* new structures of understanding, and to describe the zones of experience that are to be referred to those structures. Or, again through language and imagery, metaphors can be discovered or suggested which, though remote from the present learning situation perceptually, can be used as a ready-made skeleton of relationships on which the flesh of a new theory can be accumulated. Language increases our ability to use metaphors to construct 'models' of problematic situations, which enable us to comprehend them, and bring to bear such useful knowledge as we may have. Learners are now able to 'plant' new minitheories, as well as 'pruning' or 'cloning' existing ones.

When a problematic situation is encountered, therefore, learners can make a tacit decision whether to try to assimilate it to an existing, albeit remote, minitheory, or whether to put in the effort required to start a new 'file' from scratch. Which of these options to take depends on a variety of factors, including the weight of future experience that the theory in question is expected to have to bear, and an estimate of the relative effort required. If the expectation or the estimate is inaccurate, then learners may make the wrong choice, and find themselves in increasing difficulty. For example, if learners judge that the present difficulty is only a temporary aberration, and that normal service will be resumed shortly, and/or that accurate understanding is not too important, and/or that to set up a new file would be difficult or costly, then they are likely to decide to stick with the existing minitheory, even though it is not delivering good answers. But if, contrary to expectations, things continue in the new mould, and actually get harder, then the add-on strategy becomes increasingly unworkable. Furthermore, the opportunity to set up a new file may have been effectively missed, so they are stuck with their inadequate and fragmented way of understanding.

In general, these learning strategies, of which scientific styles of thinking comprise one potent but specialised kind, give you ideas about 'what to do when you don't know what to do'. They enable you to keep learning going, or to restart it when it has got stuck. In the area of mathematical problem-solving, for example, George Polya has identified such fall-back strategies as: 'break the problem into sub-problems'; 'create a simpler analogue of the problem and see if you can solve that'; 'try to find a visual or imaginary way of representing the problem'; or 'guess a possible solution and try to work backwards towards the answer from that'.[23] Many such strategies will be of use to the scientist too. Expert problem-solvers have so much specific knowledge and skill that most of the problems they meet are to them routine; but when they are temporarily stumped, they possess a repertoire of more general-purpose strategies such as these that can fill the gap. It may well be that the more general a strategy is, the weaker is the grasp which it gives on any particular problem; but the possession of a repertoire of them is vital if learning is not from time to time to grind to a halt.[24] Learning strategies provide a succession of 'fall-back' options which can be used to keep learning going, or to kick it back into life when it dies; and each time something promising is thrown up by such a strategy, it can be taken back into the specific domain of the problem, and worked on with greater precision.

## AWARENESS

There is one more element of scientific thinking which I have not yet referred to in this chapter: self-awareness and the ability to monitor one's own thinking and learning processes. This provides a third level of learning resource. At the most specific level are our domain-specific minitheories, equipped to deal smoothly with routine situations and minor fluctuations and deviations from them. Then there are the relatively (remember, only relatively) disembedded learning strategies, which provide a more flexible tool-kit for trying to deal with more unprecedented occurrences. But such strategies as these in their turn are far from infallible. They grind to a halt, hit unexpected snags, take longer than expected, and so on. So it is very useful to have a third level of learning power which can coordinate and take executive decisions about the learning strategies: when to persist, when to change tack, when to take a break, when to quit. This brings us to the level of 'metacognition', at which one is able to monitor and reflect on one's own learning, and take strategic decisions about how to proceed in the light of current progress and changing circumstances.[25] One asks oneself such questions as: 'what exactly am I doing?'; 'what am I trying to achieve?'; 'am I getting anywhere?'; 'is it still worth bothering?'; 'what could I be doing instead?'; 'in what ways might the analogy I am using be misleading me?'; and so on.

Several types of awareness are of use to the learner. There is the ability simply to stay focused or concentrated on a problem, despite its difficulty. There is premeditation, where one takes time to reflect on the perceived demands of a task, or to plan one's approach, before engaging with it. There is self-appraisal, in which one adjusts one's intentions in the light of one's self-knowledge – one's beliefs about how good a memory one has, and the kinds of things one finds hard to learn, for example. There is 'reflection-in-action', which involves monitoring progress and adjusting both means and ends as the work of problem solving is pursued.[26] There is reflection that is carried out in intervals between learning, or at the end of a period of struggling with a problem, where one reviews one's progress, and what one has learnt. And there is meditation, again an 'off-line' process, but involving open, alert but uncontrolled and non-focused attention, rather than the directed consciousness of problem solving.[27]

These reflective abilities, like many of the other learning strategies at the second level, develop relatively late. Both strategic and reflective capacities develop slowly, like a precious distillate, out of large bodies of domain-specific competence and understanding. This development can be fostered by education, but it cannot be directly created by instruction, for unless such strategies are rooted in the practicalities of learning and problem solving, they will not be of spontaneous utility.[28] Many people who have been through a 'study skills' course, for example, come out able to perform better on certain exercises and tests, but no more skilful as students.[29] Thus if science education wishes to address itself to the expansion of young people's ability as learners, in such a way that what is achieved will carry over into real-life learning situations, it has to take these psychological constraints into account.

## RESILIENCE

So far my description of learning and learners has been predominantly cognitive, concentrating on the structure, function and evolution of the learning mind. But the experience and performance of all learners, and especially those in school, cannot be understood in intellectual terms alone. There are, as we have seen, social influences within every learning situation, and these in turn are the source of, or are linked to, a variety of very important personal and emotional considerations. Though I am guilty in this chapter of treating these personal and emotional matters as if they could be tacked on as an afterthought, in reality nothing could be further from the truth. From the teachers' point of view, the classroom is most commonly thought of as a place where particular learning tasks make contact with a number of different brains. The goal is to help some kind of predetermined learning to occur inside a collection of individual heads. But from the learners' perspective, things are not so neat. Their overriding concern is to make sense of a complex predicament that is as much social and emotional as it is intellectual. The situation that pupils meet in a classroom is an intricate mixture of demands and opportunities. Their problem, therefore, is not to select a single strategy to respond to a single demand, but rather to develop a more general orientation towards the class, the subject and the teacher that allows them to integrate all the different kinds of constraint into a successful package of strategies for coping.[30]

In order to understand the way pupils respond to the many facets of classroom life we have to try to look at the situation they face as a whole. In particular we need to look at the ways in which the cognitive, emotional, motivational and social/cultural factors interact with each other. For the way in which individual learners approach the lesson content – the strategies they adopt towards it – will depend on their own more general goals and ambitions, their perception of the opportunities available, and on social pressures that are created by the culture of the particular class. In particular we need to be aware that pupils' engagement with the official 'content' of a lesson will be a function of the way they have decided to reconcile *all* the conflicting pressures and demands of the situation, and not merely of their 'ability' or their 'motivation'. Possessing relevant learning strategies is necessary for pupils to do well in a subject, but it is not sufficient. They must also form a central part of the overall 'game plan' that they have developed for coping with the situation. Students may be perfectly capable of learning to read, for example, but be functionally unable (or unwilling) to do so in the presence of a particular teacher or peer group.

When people encounter a new situation, one in which the best way of operating is not immediately clear, one approach is to apply learning strategies to it in the hope that understanding or mastery will result. But learning is not always the most intelligent response. Sometimes it makes better sense to decline the learning invitation and to escape from, avoid, or in some other way defend against the situation instead. These defensive strategies are as vital a set of responses to strangeness as the learning strategies. In some situations novelty may well conceal physical danger – being bitten by a dog, or run over, or beaten up. In others, more common in the classroom and staffroom, the danger may be social – a sarcastic remark from a colleague, or sniggers from other pupils when one gives a 'stupid' answer. Thus the learner's problem involves not only deciding how and what to learn about in a lesson, but also whether to engage with one of the learning opportunities at all: and if not, how to defend oneself effectively. Thus the stances that a person deploys in school may well contain defensive strategies, designed to ward off apparent threats, as well as, or instead of, learning strategies, whose function is to take up challenges.[31]

Learning in general is a risky business because it means moving out from the safety of the known into the unknown and the uncontrolled. What are these risks? The first is a loss of competence. Learners are probably going to make mistakes and errors of judgement as they explore ways of reading and dealing with novel situations. (Involved here is the ability to take criticism without becoming upset or defensive.) Second there may be a loss of clarity. The learner feels confused and at sea, without a clear mental framework within which to understand what is going on. Third there is often a loss of consistency, by which I mean learners may find themselves acting, thinking or feeling in ways that are inconsistent with their image or picture of themselves. As one experiments with different stances, for example, one may find oneself responding in ways that feel alien or out of character. And fourth, there may well be a loss of 'cool'. The learner feels intermittently anxious, frustrated, irritable or distressed. The involvement of emotion in learning, especially any learning that involves personal risks of the kinds described, is inevitable.[32]

Schooling in general, therefore, has a duty to protect and enhance students' ability to tolerate the feelings of learning, and to make sure that they are equipped to make decisions about when and how to learn as intelligently as possible. It is no use putting time and effort into teaching them how to learn if at the same time, however inadvertently, we are teaching them to be afraid of learning. Yet this is what we see in many school-leavers: a timidity and conservatism in their approach to uncertainty, which is by no means a characteristic only of the relative failures. When the successes are *addicted* to their success, they dare not experiment for fear of failure.[33]

Problems arise, and education shoots itself in the foot, when it serves to inculcate in any of its clients, beliefs about themselves and their worth which upset their balance as learners. These beliefs frequently include the following:

1. Worthwhile people do not make mistakes. Worth is contingent on competence. Incompetence is unworthy and must be paid for with guilt, shame or a loss of self-esteem.
2. Worthwhile people always know what is going on. Worth is contin-

gent on clarity. Confusion, and feeling out of control are unworthy and should be paid for with a loss of self-esteem.

3. Worthwhile people live up to, and within, their images of themselves. Worth is contingent on consistency. Acting unpredictably, out of character, or in defiance of one's precedents and principles, is unworthy and must be paid for with a loss of self-esteem.
4. Worthwhile people do not feel anxious, apprehensive, fraught or fragile. Worth is contingent on feeling cool, calm and collected. Feeling nervous, overwhelmed or spiky should be paid for with a loss of self-esteem.

What this means is that a person subject to these unconscious programming instructions will feel undermined or panicked by experiences that are necessary concomitants of many forms of learning, especially those, common at school age, that involve the learner's personality and styles of relating. Instead of being a precarious and difficult transition from a limited competence to an expanded one, the whole process can also come to feel like an assault on one's belief in oneself. People feel threatened by learning, and the rational response to perceived threat, for people as for animals, is defence. Instead of dealing with the unknown by engaging with it and mastering it (choosing a learning strategy), threatened people judge the situation too dangerous to explore, and opt instead for a strategy that is designed to preserve or maintain what they already know, or can do, or are.[34]

Sometimes such life-saving techniques are combative and assertive: students show defiance and muck about. Sometimes they lead to invisibility: students protect themselves by disappearing into the hidden wastes of average-ness.[35] And sometimes students become helpless and regressive: they publicly give up and become self-critical, dependent and upset. Research has shown that many of these children have developed a self-image in which they see themselves as confirmed 'failures', and it is this, rather than the objective truth about their capabilities as learners, that determines their helpless response.[36] It appears that once an idea like 'I am a failure' becomes embedded in a person's implicit theory about themselves it acquires the status of a self-fulfilling prophecy. If school sets up a sequence of experiences that leads students, albeit only some of them, to make such self-attributions, and therefore to become locked into a protective, rather than an exploratory, stance, then any rhetoric about 'learning to learn', or 'equipping young people to cope with uncertainty' is empty indeed. Any innovation in science education that does not see these risks clearly, and takes no effective action to avoid them, is likewise doomed to be yet another variation on the abiding theme of dissatisfaction.

## HOW IS LEARNING TO LEARN FACILITATED?

Even from this short sketch of the psychology of learning-to-learn we can see implications for education emerging. If education were truly dedicated to helping young people become good learners, it would need to start thinking in the following ways. First, there is the process of 'disembedding' to be fostered. If useful knowledge has to be grounded in an intuitive sense of what it is for, it cannot be pasted on through words, but must either crystallize out from the learners' own accumulating experience; or it must be dissolved back into that same level of knowing. The teacher's job becomes the orchestration of experience in such a way that students will be drawn towards activities that promote disembedding, and the realisation of relevance, in productive areas. In the process of solving interesting problems, such insight will accumulate, almost as a by-product.

Teachers also have to moderate the rate, as well as the quality, of experience, so that learners are not forced to run before they can walk. As it is impossible to predetermine exactly what is right for every learner every minute of the day, the only way to do this is by providing a menu of options, allowing learners some real choice, and encouraging learners to develop their own intuition about what new challenges will be suitable and productive. Approaches to the curriculum that rely on someone calculatedly deciding what a group of learners are 'ready for next' do not promote learning-to-learn, and demand an impossible degree of prescience.[37] Teachers need to be *responsive* to their students, making sure that the stepping stones are so spaced that some jump is possible for everyone, from wherever they are; and helping them to spot the most suitable jump to make.

Providing an interesting menu is vital, because without choice and responsibility, students are always likely to disengage from the learning challenge; and without the engagement of their existing stock of minitheories, there is nothing that will evolve as a result of experience. 'Being interested' is not an optional extra in this kind of learning – a sort of catalyst or turbo-charger. It is a *sine qua non*. When learning is required without engagement, it occurs in a different manner: new knowledge is hoarded alongside old, or one laminates the other, without affecting it. The evolutionary quality is lost, and without it, mental coherence and the intuitive appreciation of the value of what is discovered are lost as well.

The development of specific learning abilities can be accelerated by creating learning 'greenhouses': special contexts where problems are stylised in particular ways, and some of the real-life pressures and complexities are reduced for a while to allow greater clarity and concentration. Private music lessons, and Summer Schools do this in their different ways. But learning will not flourish when students return to real life if either their engagement has been disrupted, or their hot-house learning has not been gradually 'hardened off' – i.e. re-implanted, in an evolutionary fashion, into the real-life contexts where it is supposed to flower. Learning can be cultivated *in vitro*, but it will not show up *in vivo* unless it has been re-embedded there.

There is a role, in the promotion of learning-to-learn, for the teacher to *teach*, in the sense of imparting information and giving advice. Definitions, rules and maxims may serve the function of enabling learners to be their own coaches, reminding themselves of opportunities and ways of tackling them which then, through being acted upon, furnish their own validation. But teaching with such a goal in mind is very different from teaching content for its own sake. One has to be much more sparing with tuition, at least.

One condition which is conducive to learning-to-learn is the presence of other learners who are modelling the skills and attitudes of good learning. Teachers need to be seen to be learning themselves, and to be cheerful, absorbed, resilient and reflective learners who are capable of dealing with frustration and set-back without permanently disengaging from their chosen challenge. Science teachers, for example, would need to be seen to be genuinely engaged in their own process of discovery, and to be able to relish the uncertainties that arose.

Finally in this brief list, learning-to-learn is amplified by reflectivity – the skill, and the disposition, to apply awareness to what one is doing so that it can be better controlled and understood. Such awareness is rendered superfluous when someone else is doing the correcting and organising all the time, and it atrophies through lack of use. Conversely, reflectivity grows and strengthens on a diet of manageable responsibility – responsibility for the selection, planning, conduct, alteration, evaluation and termination of one's own learning activities. This again cannot be pre-planned, because learners differ among themselves, and from day to day, in how much responsibility they can handle, and want to. It can only be regulated by a teacher who knows the learners well, and is sensitive to their signals of interest and distress.

## MINITHEORIES AND SCHOOL SCIENCE

We saw earlier that once learners have mastered the use of metaphor and model-building, they are able to set up new minitheories from scratch to deal with situations which they see as unprecedented. I also suggested that the beneficial use of this option depends on the learner making an accurate assessment of its pros and cons, compared with the alternative of trying to treat it as an example of something more familiar; and that getting this decision wrong could be a costly mistake. This is exactly the error that many young people make with respect to school science. They approach it armed with lay understandings and informal learning strategies, and bank – perhaps with their teachers' well-intentioned encouragement – on these providing firm enough foundations on which to base the new type of learning that is required. By the time they find out that these foundations are too soft for the job, they are up a gum-tree. Let me explain this a bit more fully.

Young people have, as we have seen, some implicit theories about light, heat, gravity, evolution, outer space, atoms, biological classification, electricity, motion, chemicals, disease and so on before they encounter school science. These ideas are often just fragments of knowledge and belief, some true, some false, some contradictory, that they have picked up from sources including TV documentaries, science fiction cartoons, family myths and playground chat. Furthermore the files in which this lay knowledge is retained are not organised in any very systematic way. They are quite happily a jumble of fact, theory, opinion and value-judgement without any clear distinction; and there has been, for most young people, very little attempt to sort out any coherent theoretical infrastructure.

Additionally, the learning strategies and implicit uses of this information are not particularly systematic. Last night's *Horizon* programme may provide fodder for some good-natured arguments, but the idea of submitting its claims to sustained critical analysis, or of devising notional experiments to test its claims, is unlikely ever to occur to other than a minority of 8 or 13-year-olds. A much more prevalent *use* of information, even scientific information, is as a basis for the exploration of social relationships and social status. The file on which *Horizon* was stored is more likely to be organised around persuasion and the opportunity to test opinion than it is around the dispassionate search for truth. The quirky, funny or exciting is more germane to these activities (for many young people) than the profound or the well-researched. Even in small-group discussions of scientific topics in lessons, the view that carries the day is as likely to be that of the highest-status group member, as it is to be the most reasonable.[38]

To try to erect the formal theories of physics, for instance, on such a basis is going to be as successful as building castles on sand. The way informal knowledge is 'formatted', and the information-handling processes that are bundled with it, are just not appropriate foundations for the superstructure of rigorous, mathematical, disembodied theory that students will be required to master. As we saw in Chapter 3, the whole rigmarole of school science distances it from the knowledge, skills and interests of everyday life, and any attempt to create a flimsy bridge of content between the two, whether deliberately by the teacher, or inadvertently by the students themselves, runs the risk of misdirecting the learning process, to the particular detriment of those who are coping least well.

Ignorance of the difference in format and processing requirements of school science (as it is at present) can lead to mistakes in devising assessments. Wanting to assist pupils, especially the less able, examiners may try to cast their questions in terms of 'real-life' events or situations. An assessment of understanding of the forces of gravity and friction, for example, may be couched in terms of children playing on a water-slide. The assumption is that increasing the 'familiarity' of the content will facilitate the retrieval of relevant information and operations from the pupils' minds. However what the well-intentioned examiner has done is to create a problem that is even more *un*usual from the students' point of view – for their experience of water-slides has absolutely no connection with the conscious and deliberate application of quantitative physical principles. The conjunction of an out-of-school content with an in-school kind of process (doing calculations, estimating magnitudes or whatever) may be very confusing, especially for the so-called 'less able'. Thus the net effect of the intention to make a test 'fairer' is to further handicap the least successful.

Students are faced with a dilemma. If they opt to try to tack their increasingly logical, mathematical, intellectual school science on to existing minitheories that relate to the physical world, they are not going to find in those modules the learning resources they are going to need, and consequently their understanding is likely to be dis-integrated and superficial – a few rote-learned definitions and some flotsam and jetsam left behind from practical classes. However much their potential for tidy logical construction, they will be faced with the same problem that a person would be if, while working on a 100-piece jigsaw puzzle of the Eiffel Tower, they were being handed bits that actually belonged to a 1000-piece puzzle of Constable's *Haywain*. All they can do is collect them.

On the other hand, if they set up a new domain, separate from the world of everyday activities and discussions, labelled 'Physics', they may, if they are successful, pass their exams, but the effective mental apartheid they have created ensures that there will be little transfer back to the 'real world'. It is this Catch 22 that underlies much of the dissatisfaction that we reviewed in Chapter 2. Even if curriculum developers try to write student-friendly texts, with examples about skate-boarding and playing video games, the underlying demand for coherence, mathematisation, hypothetico-deductive thinking and the ability to rationalise and articulate all one's theories and beliefs, irrevocably mark school science off from everyday life for the majority of students, and force them onto the horns of this dilemma. The skate-boarding is going to make the whole thing more, not less, confusing. And at that point the third alternative, finding a way to escape, starts to look very attractive – switch off, go invisible, muck about, pretend it doesn't matter. Redirect your attention to areas of experience that you *can* actually make some sense of: the playful possibilities of gas-taps and woodlice, or the budding relationship between Jayne and Brendan. While the venerable abstractions of traditional school science remain at the heart of the secondary curriculum, there is a sense of 'damned if you do (try to link them to out-of-school contexts), and damned if you don't'.

DEVELOPMENTAL TRAJECTORIES

Children start out with some basic learning equipment which is then developed and expanded through their interactions with their worlds. At first they are 'scientists' of an effective, but compared with science proper, only a primitive kind. Their knowledge, viewed from 'outside', is exceedingly patchy and unsystematic. It is intuitive and tacit: children do not know what they know. And it is essentially practical, and tied to the first-hand scenarios of the child's personal world. Its evolution is driven by the changing flux of personal concerns – concerns that are predominantly biological and social. Experiments are impulsive and small-scale, constantly nibbling away at the edges of the unknown, like a caterpillar eating a leaf, but unable to take larger or better-planned bites.

The way in which the mind develops is constrained by its basic architecture, and by universal features of the environment which it is trying to comprehend. But the social and physical peculiarities of its surroundings will, whether they have been deliberately planned by adults or not, channel its development in one way or another. And education, we might say, represents a culture's attempt to influence the development of mind deliberately, constructing a trellis of ideas and exercises along which mental growth can be persuaded to train itself. Different aims and values will require different kinds of trelliswork to harness and guide the evolution of the mind's powers. Thus science educators, for example, must plan their instructional climbing frame in the light of both the intrinsic nature of the material they are trying to train, and the endpoint they are seeking to achieve.

If science education is to be aimed at the production of scientists proper, then it has to influence the growth of mind in a variety of different ways. Where there was a happy jumble of purpose-built minitheories, there should instead be coherence and generality. Where minitheories were originally composed of working knowledge, largely tacit and experiential, the goal of the scientist is to construct theories that are consciously conceived and articulate. Where experiments were driven by personal need, they now have to become disconnected from what the scientist wants or believes. Where intuitive science was firmly embedded in a vital, rich and long-standing social context, scientists proper find themselves in a very different kind of social scene. Science education finds itself faced with the task of training the mind's development in directions many of which are the very antitheses of those which 'came naturally'.

By the time they are 10-years-old or so, most young people have moved closer to the prescription of the 'scientist' that we created in the last chapter; but they are still some considerable cognitive distance away. They are up to a point able to articulate their ideas, ask pertinent questions, offer critical comment, see the relationship between a prediction and an experiment, suggest explanations for physical phenomena. But the logic remains shaky, the articulation ragged, the distinction between observation, explanation and personal judgement sporadic, the ability to concentrate on problems that seem to lack any personal contact point, weak. They are, usually at best, *informal* scientists.

Science demands above all, as we saw in the last chapter, commitment to a style of thinking; and this, like all other learning skills, must evolve from earlier forms of thought. Scientific thinking is a development, a refinement, of everyday types of thinking; but if science education *presupposes* it, choosing to worry instead about the topics and the lab skills to teach, and does not concern itself with how to *train* it, then it is going to continue to present to many young people an unbridgeable gap between school science and the real world. The more pressing problem is: how to develop scientific thinking in such a way that young people are able to carry it out into their everyday problem-solving, and use it when it is appropriate?[39]

## NOTES

[1] See Joseph Novak and Bob Gowin, *Learning How to Learn*, CUP: Cambridge, 1984.

[2] My book *Teaching to Learn: A direction for education*, Cassell: London, 1990 is an attempt to sketch such a psychology. Many of the arguments in this chapter are developed more fully in that book, and it may be useful to consult at points where this chapter becomes rather condensed.

[3] See George Kelly, *The Psychology of Personal Constructs*, Norton: New York, 1955; D. Bannister and F. Fransella, *Inquiring Man*, 3rd edition, Croom Helm: Beckenham, 1987.

[4] By, for example, Rosalind Driver, *The Pupil as Scientist*, Open University Press: Milton Keynes, 1983; Roger Osborne and Peter Freyberg, *Learning in Science*, Heinemann: Auckland, 1985.

[5] See the chapters by Vicki Bruce, 'Perceiving', and by Nigel Harvey, 'The psychology of action: current controversies', in Guy Claxton (ed.), *Growth Points in Cognition*, Routledge: London, 1988.

[6] For example, Arthur Lucas and Paul Black (eds), *Children's Implicit Ideas in Science*, Routledge: London, 1991.

[7] For reviews of these beliefs, see Rosalind Driver, Edith Guesne and Andree Tibergien (eds), *Children's Ideas in Science*, Open University Press: Milton Keynes, 1985.

[8] See Guy Claxton, 'Cognition doesn't matter if you're scared, depressed or bored', in Philip Adey (ed.), *Adolescent Development and School Science* , Falmer: London, 1989.

[9] This is discussed much more fully in my *Teaching to Learn, op. cit.* See also Marvin Minsky, *The Society of Mind*, Pan: London, 1988; and Roger Schank, *Explanation Patterns*, Erlbaum: Hillsdale, NJ, 1986.

[10] This outline is, from a psychological point of view, crude in the extreme. Many important areas of current uncertainty and controversy will be glossed over. However my intention here is not to present a theory of development, but merely to exemplify the way the 'minitheory' concept can be used. Some of the psychological background can be found in Jerome Bruner and Helen Haste, *Making Sense: The child's construction of the world*, Methuen: London, 1987; and Gavin Bremner, *Infancy*, Blackwell: Oxford, 1988.

[11] The notion of 'attunement' comes from Daniel Stern, *The Interpersonal World of the Child*, Basic Books: New York, 1985.

[12] See Margaret Donaldson's classic *Children's Minds*, Fontana: London, 1978, and also her chapter, 'The origins of inference', in Bruner and Haste, *op. cit.*

[13] See Schank, *op. cit.*

[14] When children's early social development is disrupted, for example if the mother is rendered unresponsive through suffering from post-natal depression, their cognitive development may be retarded for several years: see Colwyn Trevarthen, 'Instincts for human understanding and for cultural cooperation: their dependency in infancy', in M. von Cranach, K. Foppa, W. Lepenies and D. Ploog (eds), *Human Ethology: claims and limits of a new discipline*, CUP: 1979; and Lynne Murray, 'The infant's role in mother-infant communications', *Journal of Child Language*, 1986, **13**, 15–29.

[15] See Judy Deloache and Ann Brown, 'The early emergence of planning skills', in Bruner and Haste, *op. cit.*

[16] See Margaret Carr and Guy Claxton, 'The costs of calculation', *New Zealand Journal of Educational Studies*, 1989, **24**, 129–40.

[17] Deloache and Brown, *op. cit.*

[18] For more details, see my *Teaching to Learn, op. cit.*

[19] Maybe a better analogy is with Bruner's 'enactive' and 'iconic' stages—see Jerome Bruner, *Towards a Theory of Instruction*, Harvard University Press: Cambridge MA, 1966.

[20] Warning: this section is especially speculative.

[21] Here I am following the approach of Vygotsky, which is exciting much current interest. See L. S. Vygotsky, *Mind in Society*, Harvard University Press: Cambridge MA, 1978.

[22] Daniel Dennett, *Elbow Room: The Varieties of Free Will Worth Wanting*, Clarendon Press: Oxford, 1984.

[23] George Polya, *How to Solve it*, Anchor-Doubleday: Garden City NY, 1954.

[24] This has also been suggested by David Perkins and Gavriel Salomon, 'Are cognitive skills context-bound?', *Educational Researcher*, 1989, **18**, 16–25.

[25] See John Nisbett and Janet Shucksmith, *Learning Strategies*, RKP: London, 1986.

[26] Donald Schon, *The Reflective Practitioner*, Basic Books: New York, 1983.

[27] See my chapter 'Buddhist psychology', and others, in Michael West (ed.), *The Psychology of Meditation*, Clarendon Press: 1987.

[28] Still one of the best discussions of this is Michael Polanyi's *Personal Knowledge*, RKP: London, 1958.

[29] Nisbett and Shucksmith, *op. cit.*

[30] These 'stances' are discussed at length, and exemplified, in my *Teaching to Learn, op. cit.*

[31] See for example Don Hamachek, *Encounters with the Self*, 3rd edition, Holt Rinehart and Winston: Chichester, 1987.

[32] I go into this in more detail in my *Live and Learn*, Open University Press: Milton Keynes, 1988.

[33] This very important work is due to Carol Dweck. See for example her 'Motivational processes affecting learning', *American Psychologist*, 1986, **41**, 1040–8; and 'The power of negative thinking', *Times Educational Supplement*, 21 September 1984, p.21.

[34] See for example Martin Hammersley and Peter Woods (eds), *Life in Schools: The Sociology of Pupil Culture*, Open University Press: Milton Keynes, 1984.

[35] For a poignant account of these children, see James Pye's *Invisible Children*, OUP: Oxford, 1988.

[36] Dweck, *op. cit.*

[37] See Carr and Claxton, *op. cit.*

[38] See Joan Solomon, 'The social construction of school science', in Millar, *op. cit.*

[39] For further reading on the psychology of learning, I would recommend Nisbet and Shucksmith's *Learning Strategies, op. cit.*, and my own *Teaching to Learn, op. cit.*.More general surveys are provided by Michael Howe's *A Teacher's Guide to the Psychology of Learning*, Blackwell: Oxford, 1984; and David Fontana's *Psychology for Teachers*, 2nd edition, British Psychological Society/Methuen: London, 1988. The involvement of 'self' in learning is well documented by Robert Burns' *Self-Concept Development and Education*, Holt, Rinehart and Winston: Eastbourne, 1982. For approaches to the specific problems of learning science, Richard White's *Learning Science, op. cit.*, is the best thing available.

# CHAPTER SIX

———————— · ————————

# WHAT ARE WE TEACHING SCIENCE FOR?

Science in the modern world has many uses; its chief use, however, is to provide long words to cover the errors of the rich. The word 'kleptomania' is a vulgar example of what I mean.

G. K. Chesterton

In this chapter I am going to try to pull together some of the threads and arguments that have emerged from the preceding discussions, and apply them to the question of what science education might be in aid of. My intention is to spell out some of the options that are, or that have seemed to be, available, and to see what it is that they really involve, and what conditions would be necessary to achieve them. I shall try here to pull apart some common composite goals in order to clarify the demands of their constituents; and to suggest some additional ones. Having laid out in some detail what school science *could* be about, I shall then begin to argue a case for what it *should* aim towards: to select from amongst what is practicable on the basis of some value judgements about what is preferable.

It might be useful to clarify, before we start, what role the discussion of the last chapter has in this. Psychology, being itself a kind of scientific venture, does not indicate directly what our priorities ought to be, as far as educational objectives are concerned. But by analysing the way young people learn, it can show what learning options may be available; what conditions will facilitate or impede the achievement of those options; which options may be pursued simultaneously and which, needing different kinds of soil in which to grow, may be incompatible. Psychology helps us build a description of what is *possible*, and only in the light of this can we make informed and realistic choices about what is *desirable*.

THE AIMS OF SCIENCE EDUCATION

### 'To transmit scientific knowledge'

One venerable (in the dual sense of both respectable and traditional) aim is to inform young people about what scientists proper have found out. It has been argued, by the C.P. Snow/R.S. Peters school of philosophy, that science constitutes an intrinsically worthwhile body of knowledge, an important strand of our culture, and that nobody should be considered 'educated', in our present society, unless they are aware of at least the fundamentals of this knowledge.[1]

This aim is perfectly coherent and defensible as far as it goes, but it is incompletely specified. It is couched in terms of 'knowledge', 'under-standing' and 'awareness', but it does not tell us how these are to be recognised. Boringly behaviouristic though it sounds, aims of education have to be specified in terms of observable differences from something or other, or we are unable to say whether, and to what extent, they have been achieved. This is a nuisance when the aim one wants to achieve is an intellectual one of this kind, because the performance that tends to be accepted by default, as a necessary evil, is that of some kind of written exam. But this, as is now well-known, is not 'neutral' with respect to the expectations, purposes and demands which it lodges in students' minds: the anticipated 'test' creates a disposition to learn in particular ways, and these are not always conducive to establishing the 'mental grasp' which perhaps was the original goal.[2] Presumably Sir Charles Snow did not just want students to be able to recite the Second Law of Thermodynamics like parrots; he wanted them to understand something of the conceptual framework which gave birth to it, and of its use and implications. And also, equally well-known, is the fact that taking written exams is a skilled performance, so that differences in scores reflect an inseparable combina-tion of what has been 'learnt', and this specialised facility, which is incidental to the original aim.

Thus any goal that is couched in academic terms runs the risk of having its intentions contaminated when it comes down to the nitty-gritty of assessment. The only way to avoid this trap is to specify more clearly in the beginning what it is that you want students to be able to *do*, and then to target any examination of achievement on that identified performance. This is fairer to students, more valid, and truer to the psychology which we sketched in the last chapter. The minitheory perspective requires us to give up the idea that 'knowledge' is a general-purpose, homogeneous mental commodity, ready to turn its hand instantly to any kind of task to which it is potentially relevant. Minitheories are purpose-built, and that means that things are learnt in the light of anticipated uses. The vaguer the sense of anticipation, or the more a test deviates from what was predicted, the less right we have to expect instant competence.

However, teaching with the dominant aim of getting as many of your students as possible through a chemistry exam (rather than getting them to *understand* chemistry) is also a perfectly valid intention to have. One could argue that the possession of passes in public exams is a greater potential enhancer of the quality of life than an accurate understanding of some venerable scientific concepts, and that therefore if these two aims diverge, teaching for the test is the one to stick with. As I said, doing tests in science or any other subject is a performance more skilled and specific than doing a back-flip on the four-inch beam, and if one wants people to be good at it, why then one should give them plenty of training and coaching. This hard-headed attitude is usually disparaged as 'cramming' or 'cheating' by teachers who do not consider exam performance to be the be-all and end-all of school, but who cling to the fond but illicit belief that success in exams *must* somehow reflect at least a measure of genuine understanding.

If one espouses the transmission aim wholeheartedly, then traditional teaching methods – chalk and talk, dictating notes, mock exams, etc. – may well turn out to be the most effective, at least for those students who are up to it.[3] It is quite possible, despite all the 'discovery learning' hype of the last two decades, that clear explanations and teacher demonstrations 'get the stuff across' better than methods that are more practical or social. There is certainly no need to try to make your teaching method mimic some idealised image of the process of scientific discovery itself. Pretending to students that you want them to find out what other people have already established as 'correct' is, as we saw in Chapter 2, a sure way of confusing them. The didactic teacher can escape from this particular ambivalence.

A perennial problem with the 'transmission of knowledge' aim, though, is that there is so much knowledge to transmit that it is hard to know what to put in and what to leave out. Teachers have sometimes blamed the university-dominated examination boards, or the College Examination Entrance Board, for stuffing the science syllabuses with prescribed topics. Yet members of those same boards complain that when they try to clear some space, there is always a howl of protest from somebody about the threatened deletion of their 'favourite' block of work.[4] The same sense of arbitrariness hangs over many current attempts at reform, which despite including some issues of modern concern – 'the greenhouse effect', information technology – is still dominated by traditional wodges of Phys, Chem and Bio. Why there is nothing in the National Curriculum for England and Wales explicitly on the human central nervous system (unless you count the good old 'structure and function of the eye'), and the amazing advances over the last twenty years in the understanding of the brain, is a mystery.

The selection of topics, especially in physics, seems to be premised on the assumption that there is a core of vital concepts which absolutely has to be mastered before any significant progress can be made in more specific, or perhaps more up-to-date areas: without 'energy' and 'force' you really will not be able to get very far. It may be that this is true, but I doubt it, and remain to be convinced. Or it may be that these concepts, and their associated 'demonstrations' are to physical science what Shakespeare is to English: they deserve their pride of place because of their historical influence and their cultural importance. Again I wait to be persuaded that this claim should be preferred to the many others which we are going to review. And if the main motive for teaching science is to develop certain ways of thinking and learning, then there is even less reason to force students to 'practise' on concepts that are so abstract and remote. It is a reasonable suspicion that much of the content of the science curriculum has survived the recent shake-ups because of inertia, vested interests, and an unwillingness on the part of paymasters to commit the necessary funds to the considerable amount of retraining and reorganisation that would be involved, not because of its unanswerable case for inclusion.

Whether content is being taught for exam success or for its intrinsic value, two questions, apart from what precisely to teach, loom over this intention. First, can this goal be effectively achieved without sacrificing or jeopardising other desirable objectives? Second, is this an appropriate goal for *all* young people, or might there not be more pressing claims on the time that is dedicated to science education? As we go on to discuss some of these competing claims, it will begin to look increasingly as if the answer to both these questions is No. The concern to 'get the stuff over' certainly often seems to work against *other* aims that one might wish to have for science education – such as developing young people's own inquisitiveness, and skill in learning; or giving them an accurate picture of how scientific knowledge is really created. As Robin Millar says:

> if teaching science is really the transmission of a body of consensually accepted knowledge, what is its value as general education? Is there a role for personal enquiry and investigation?. . .Most science educators would, rightly, see significant potential dangers in teaching textbook science. . .The *pedagogical* danger is that teaching becomes an arid business of rote learning of standard facts, theories and methods. The *epistemological* danger is that it makes science look like infallible, received knowledge.[5]

*'To improve young people's personal theories about the world, so that they shall make better sense of it, and therefore act on it more effectively'*

A variation on the theme of 'content', currently much in vogue, says that it is useful to people to know some of the scientists' theories, because these theories have stood the test of time and careful investigation, and are therefore better, more valid or more accurate, than the implicit beliefs and understandings picked up from everyday life. Obviously life will work better with better theories. This view has been propounded particularly by those who have been most active in uncovering what these flawed, proto-scientific myths are. Take these three snippets from Osborne and Freyberg, for example. 'As teachers we would want at least some children to exchange their existing ideas for those of scientists.' 'The aim of science education is to enable learners to make better sense of their world by helping them restructure their ideas in useful and useable ways.' And: 'The teaching task is to ascertain individual children's conceptions about science topics and to modify these towards the current scientific view.'[6] Again it is not very clear exactly *why* it is so good for 'children' to swap their ideas for those of science proper – what precisely will they be able to do, or do better, with those ideas than without them? Well, 'make better sense of their world', I suppose; though people seem to make the sense that matters quite well without having studied science. Christian fundamentalists may be well out of step with current science in denying the theory of evolution by natural selection, but it is not clear that their misapprehension 'handicaps' them in any way. Indeed, to believe what your community believes is often a functional thing to do, and one which the *scientific* community is as 'guilty' of as the rest of us.

The question here is: in what ways exactly are scientific theories 'better' than lay ones? Remember that science has more criteria by which to judge a theory than just its predictive accuracy: scientific theories are also preferred if they are comprehensive, parsimonious, quantitative and consistent with more general assumptions that form part of the scientific world-view. Scientific theories also have to be *expressed* in an articulate, formal, logical fashion. None of these additional criteria need apply to the theories that people use to guide them through daily life. It is perfectly all right to have a patchwork of local theories, rather than one great big one – indeed the psychology of Chapter 5 tells us that such minitheories are the mental 'norm'. It is quite all right for some of our theories to be over-elaborated, or approximate, or intuitive: it is whether they *work*, whether they support our human goals, that matters, not how elegant or clever they are. Newtonian dynamics may be a pretty neat way of describing the motion of solid bodies, but nobody was ever chucked out of a football team because they didn't understand it. Our 'gut theory' of force, speed and movement is more use to us, even to ice skaters, for getting around our everyday world, even though it is limited *to* that world. And if our interests or occupations require us to master a more formal theory, we would in many cases be advised to learn it 'as well', rather than 'instead of'.

Part of the confusion is created by the demand of science education to *articulate* everything. It could not really avoid it, as it is an obsession that both its parents, Science and Education, share. But when young people are asked to discuss their 'ideas' about burning or floating, they are being asked to do something very difficult, for the (quite sophisticated) minitheories that comprise their knowledge about these phenomena are not designed to talk. They were built to guide successful interactions with fire and water, and students may have had no need, up to the moment when the teacher makes this strange request, to add a commentary. In fact psychological research has shown that the minitheory that offers explanations of something is frequently *different* from the one that guides our non-verbal dealings with it.[7]

Thus when teachers or researchers ask young people to articulate their ideas about some natural phenomenon, the observers may not be witnessing the students' 'implicit theories' at all, but only the common rationalisations that they cobble together when they are put on the spot: ideas that may well be 'generated in an *ad hoc* way in response to the social pressure to produce an answer in an interview or test situation'.[8] This means that we should be very wary of attributing to young people firm but false conceptions which it is our duty to root out and replace with better ones. But we do not need to be too worried: attempts to persuade these transplants to occur, whether by the 'soft' method of discussion and discovery, or the 'hard' one of forcible confrontation with the 'superiority' of the scientific view, have proved generally unsuccessful, a testament not to students' 'stubbornness' but to the very real and effective power of their pre-existing tacit models of the world (whatever they happened to contain). Science educators of this persuasion have been guilty of treating young people in the way that missionaries treat 'savages'. They should perhaps be grateful that they have been treated in return more leniently than the savages have a reputation for treating *their* saviours.

One more point needs making about the relation between intellectual ideas and the control of spontaneous behaviour – what have been called 'espoused theories' as opposed to 'theories-in-action'.[9] As I have said espoused theories often lie alongside our theories-in-action without influencing them, splitting us between two centres, one mental and reflective, the other behavioural and impulsive. But espoused theories, things we have been taught, *can* come to influence our spontaneous reactions and intuitions if they are used in reflective moments while we are working on some learning task. They can act as a stored set of maxims and reminders which we can use to check and guide our learning when we hit snags. They are the voice of an internalised coach. The problem is that, unless the habit of pausing while we are actually 'on-task', and inviting the coach to contribute, has become second nature, whatever useful knowledge we *potentially* have will not come to bear on the practical activity. It will remain, as it so often does, tied to contexts of acquisition, and disembedded (and disembodied) discussion. Thus having been taught a theory that is of potential use to some area of practical activity may be a necessary, but it is certainly not a sufficient, condition for that theory to make a difference. Unless learners have also developed the habit of *reflection*-in-action then such knowledge will remain 'merely' intellectual. I shall return to the possibility of education as the cultivation of a reflective disposition in a little while.

For this aim of science education to become a practicable and a valuable one, therefore, three conditions have to be fulfilled. First, whatever theories are offered have to be cast in the form of 'working knowledge'; hints and insights that can be brought to bear on practical activity. It is no use offering a watered-down version of a scientific view of the world, and vaguely hoping that it will somehow make a difference to the quality of life. Such a move would constitute a bogus rationale for retaining science lessons much as they are – while adding another source of potential guilt for students (or the conscientious ones at any rate) when they find that they are unable to extract the practical value that they are being told is there. It is seductive, and like all seductions, confusing to the victims.

The second requirement is for these working theories, when they have been formulated, to be introduced in the context of reflective problem solving. Teaching has to be structured in such a way that:

1. Students are working on a problem with their existing learning strategies and minitheories.
2. These existing resources are proving inadequate.
3. Information or advice is introduced sparingly into this predicament.
4. Students are then given time to find out for themselves whether it helps or not.
5. On subsequent occasions, they are encouraged to check their own mental notice-board for handy tips when they get stuck.

This sort of teaching is like making mayonnaise: it is vital that you add your knowledge and guidance drop by drop, allowing the learners to beat it into the consistency of their own active minitheories. Any impatience on the teachers' part and the learning will curdle: what you have added will separate out and will no longer be embedded in the spontaneous approaches that students make to their problems. It will go back to being intellectual. Until these conditions are met, calls for science teaching to effect change in students' real-life competence will be counter productive.

Third, as we saw at length in Chapter 3, the whole set-up of the science lesson has to approach much more closely the conditions of everyday life

if the understanding and skill that is acquired there is to show up spontaneously as students pursue their out-of-school lives.

A much grander claim for the improvement of common sense by the study
of science has been made by Paul Churchland, an American philosopher
of science.[10] His starting point is the 'theory-ladenness' of our perception,
which we discussed in Chapter 4. Not only are scientists constrained to
look at the world through their theoretical preconceptions: so are we all.
The very observations we all make are influenced by the theoretical view
of the world into which our culture has inducted us, and to which we are
tacit subscribers. Our perceptions, he says:

> are rooted, in substantial measure, not in the nature of our perceptual environ-
> ment, nor in the innate features of our psychology, but rather in the structure
> and content of our common language, and in the process by which each child
> acquires the normal use of that language. By this process, each of us grows into
> a conformity with the current conceptual template. In large measure we *learn*,
> from others, to perceive the world as everyone else perceives it. But if this is so,
> then we might have learnt, and may yet learn, to conceive/perceive the world
> in ways other than those supplied by our present culture. After all, our current
> conceptual framework is just the latest stage in the long evolutionary process
> that produced it, and we may examine with profit the possibility that perception
> might take place within the matrix of a different and more powerful conceptual
> framework.
>
> The obvious candidate here is the conceptual framework of modern physical
> theory – of physics, chemistry and their many satellite sciences. That the
> conceptual framework of these sciences is immensely powerful is beyond
> argument, and its credentials as a systematic representation of reality are unpar-
> alleled. It must be a dull man indeed whose appetite will not be whet by the
> possibility of perceiving the world directly in its terms. . .
>
> If our perceptual judgements must be laden with theory in any case, then why
> not have them laden with the best theory available?..the resulting expansion of
> our perceptual consciousness would be profound. Should we ever succeed in
> making the shift, we shall be properly at home in our physical universe for the
> very first time.

Here is a radical programme for science education indeed. If the very
world we appear to inhabit is a product of our adherence to an out-of-date
scientific view; and if it is archaic because of the slow rate of diffusion out
of the laboratory into our common language, and thence into our common
sense – then school science becomes the ideal place to feed into the
diffusion process an up-to-date set of ideas, and to speed it up. But note
that this is at best a long-term project. Our way of seeing is not automatically changed as a result of instruction or information, any more than our
way of acting is. As Churchland says, the new viewpoint has to become
part of the way we speak, not just another topic of conversation, before it
comes to exert any hold over perception. I conclude that, while this may

be an interesting possibility, it is too remote to do more than place some pressure on the science curriculum to be as modern as possible – and this is already desirable, for a number of other reasons.

### 'To make young people better learners'

I have already moved, in the last section, from the 'content'-dominated view of science education to the 'process' view. There have been many claims recently that school science is well-equipped to enhance students' ability to be good real-life learners. Dick White, for instance says that science education 'should assist all to maintain an eagerness and an ability to find out all that they can about their world, throughout life. . .education in science should develop in students responsibility for their own learning and strategies that are applied in the acquisition and comprehension of knowledge.'[11] Here the claim spills over any bounds of content: science education is to become nothing less than the main vehicle whereby we Enhance Effective Learning.[12]

Now we reviewed in the last chapter some of the conditions that are required for the fulfilment of this aim. Basically the teachers' job becomes that of creating an environment that is varied and challenging enough to accelerate the growth and disembedding of learning skills; offering a model to students of a self-confident and skilful learner; and interacting with students in such a way that nothing is done to undermine their (the students') willingness to take on learning challenges or their belief in their own capability to learn. For reasons that I have discussed elsewhere,[13] the reorganisation of education along these lines is a long-term project. Though there are those (myself included) who think that some such transformation is vital, its achievement is not helped by holding out the hope that substantial progress towards it can be made by individuals working on their own teaching methods within the present structure. Teachers who are drawn towards such an objective find it, however committed they are to start with, an uphill struggle against the constraints of time, syllabus and expectations from all around them, not least the students. Against such odds, it is very common for them to lapse regretfully back into more traditional ways, or to leave schoolteaching for a less constricting working context. Teachers who are already dissatisfied with the job they are doing become even more confused when educationalists write books suggesting that they could teach for learning *at the same time* as persisting with the existing goals and procedures.[14]

What teachers say, and indeed often what they intend, is that science should be about finding things out for yourself, and, in the process, learning to become a more skilful finder-outer. With some orchestration by the teacher, students ask ever more sophisticated questions of Nature, and

Nature answers back. Yet as soon as it becomes tangled up with the agenda of the official curriculum, the rhetoric takes second place to quite a different reality. However well teachers try to conceal their knowledge or their impatience, it soon becomes clear to students that their well-intentioned observations and questions are treated as frequently being wide of some invisible mark which, nevertheless, they are somehow supposed to be able to see or sense.

When sensible attempts to participate meet such a mystifying and recurrent lack of enthusiasm, many students quickly learn that the best thing to do is act dumb and wait for teachers to answer their own questions – which they inevitably will. The current dis-ease of science teachers leads some of them to turn their lessons into a charade in which first they encourage students to express their own thoughts, then offer an experiment whilst pretending not to know the outcome, and finally dictate the 'conclusion', which is, you remember, 'where we write down what should have happened'. In this Kafkaesque situation, some students learn how to play along, some flounder gamely, some wait quietly to be shown or told, and others escape from the mental discomfort of not knowing what the hell is going on by mucking about.

There is no way round it: you simply cannot teach science as real-life empowerment and science as received wisdom at the same time, and in the same way. To try to do so is to create false hopes and double-binds. If we want to teach an accepted set of concepts and procedures, then there are right and wrong answers; good and bad experiments; relevant and irrelevant observations; appropriate and inappropriate use of concepts. Education in this mode becomes a training and an induction, and teachers must provide evaluative feedback if they are to do the job required. The point of the practical is *not* to find out what happens: it is to illustrate a principle, or to learn how to do a 'clean' experiment – and that is one which gives the answer in the book.[15] For young people who wish to join the community of professional scientists, such an apprenticeship is vital and valid. For everyone else it is not clear that it warrants compulsory attendance for a substantial amount of time.

Thus there are many reasons why the aim of using school science to enhance young people's ability as real-life learners and problem solvers, however desirable, is not at present a valid option. The ways in which the school science laboratory is typically structured, materially, socially and educationally, strongly militate against such an ambition. It is impossible to simulate the conditions of real-life problem solving in school, given the constraints of time, syllabus, types of communication and inevitable teacher-domination which exist. Thus the bridge is not made, and the traffic never flows. To help young people become good learners requires both more and less than school science currently offers. More in the sense of ways of learning and thinking that are not scientific, and an appreciation that scientific thinking is a valuable *and limited* component of a much larger repertoire. Less in the sense of less impatience to present all the putative goodies that science has to offer.

### 'To train routine scientists'

As we have just seen, one clear, practicable aim of science education is to produce, or start on the production of, the routine scientists that will staff the research and development labs of industry and the funded projects of universities and polytechnics. Some consider this to be the be-all and end-all of science education. Michael Young, for example, says:

> Science teaching began and continues with its main purpose to maintain the supply of future scientists. This has two interrelated and in effect self-justifying outcomes – the mass scientific and technological ignorance of a people in an increasingly technologically dominated society, who see themselves as dependent on experts in more and more aspects of their lives; and a community of scientists who see the knowledge which they are responsible for producing and validating as necessarily not available to the community at large.[16]

For Young the goal of producing working scientists is clearly achieved at unacceptable costs: the creation of a split between an elite who are the custodians and governors of science, and the rest of us, who are prevented by a variety of means, not least our sense of our own inability to 'understand', from having any access to, or control over, this power source. School science as it is currently practised seems almost deliberately designed to be so 'hard' and unappealing that most people will gain a conditioned aversion to it, like Pavlov's dogs, and will be quite happy to leave its management to the minority who have survived the difficult initiation tests. To make it more 'relevant' or 'accessible' therefore would undermine this balance on which technological societies depend, and would be opposed by those who profit by the current situation. While there are undoubtedly those who do gain advantage from having a scientifically illiterate and depowered population – proponents of the nuclear power industry, or manufacturers of dangerous drugs and fertilisers, perhaps – I tend to prefer a 'cock-up' explanation for the state of school science to a 'conspiracy' one, and therefore retain some optimism about the ability of reasoned argument to bring about significant improvement.

The much more straightforward question about the aim of preparing young people to be routine scientists concerns its place as a compulsory part of the school curriculum. If an induction into the procedures and working concepts of the professional scientist cannot be defended as a 'training of the mind' – as I have argued it cannot – then why should it form a more important part of the school curriculum than training for any other specific vocation: piloting a jumbo jet, or offset printing, for example?

If science education is to be primarily a training, then it does not help that aim to pretend it is also an 'education' – in just the same way that the ambivalence about teacher training/teacher education has created confusion. In training, initiative and critical analysis of what you are doing are necessary only in so far as they contribute to your ability to do the job you are being prepared for. That may be considerable or it may be minimal, and the form of the training should vary accordingly. In the case of routine science, as we saw in Chapter 4, the major requirements are good working knowledge of the relevant technical literature, and the skill and disposition to carry out experimental tests meticulously. If much of the current practical-based science curriculum were to give up the pretence that it is also about the creation of ideas, and personal inquiry, and were to up-date its knowledge base and introduce more technological applications, then it would not be doing a bad job of hitting this target. The only trouble is that not all young people need or want such a training.

School science varies in the extent to which it tries to have it both ways. Sometimes the rhetoric of inquiry and discovery is at odds with the reality of foregone conclusions and right observations. Sometimes the rhetoric is missing, and students at least know where they stand. Jane French, in a study of 11-year-olds' initiation into secondary science lessons, found that, 'while pupils may well acquire a taste of what it is like to be a professional scientist, there is, in these data at least, no pretence that they are "real scientists" engaged in real discovery.'[17] Many young people's experience is not nearly so clear-cut. The Science working party for the new National Curriculum for England and Wales introduced the section on practical activities with the sentence 'Exploring and investigating is [sic] central to the work of scientists and science education'.[18] Here the intention is obviously that students should be 'finding out' as well as 'learning how'.

### *'To be frontier scientists'*

It is a different thing to want school science to produce frontier scientists. As we saw in Chapter 4, these are much more troublesome, less controllable people. It is their job to ask embarrassing questions about the presuppositions – and even the values – on which a scientific investigation is based. Though we might say that we want to foster the development of such people, in practice it is their nature to be difficult, disruptive and a damn nuisance. A few might be an asset; a lot are a liability. Thus if we are thinking in terms of social or economic criteria, a regular supply of routine scientists is a higher priority than the encouragement of people to be independent, deep, creative thinkers.

In fact, the training regime that produces routine scientists works against the development of the essential qualities of the frontier scientist. Frontier scientists are more interested in questions than answers; more intrigued by what has been taken as read than how to patch up a specific conjecture or solve a technical problem. They are often more comfortable working alone than in a team. They are happy to wait in the dark for the light to dawn; they do not have to rush around looking for a candle and matches.[19] Of course they will need their lab technique, their mathematical skill, and their ability to write a clear, convincing paper, eventually. But they need to have acquired these without the requisite discipline having rubbed out their creativity: the trained rationality must not have overwhelmed the educated intuition. And in school it often does. Take the example of learning to write in the formally prescribed 'scientific' manner. Clive Sutton points out the danger.

> If you are learning to be a scientist, the presentation of evidence to a critical public is an important part of your craft, and so the system (of writing as in a scientific paper) is appropriate where the purpose of science education is apprenticeship. . .but in school the suppression of first thoughts, conjectures, preliminary beliefs, hopes or reasons for doing an experiment could be both a misrepresentation of science and an interruption in the development of the learner's own thought.[20]

The abilities of the frontier scientist are in some ways like those of the 'good learner' (though we should not push the analogy too far: scientists, remember, are bound to be articulate, logical and comprehensive, while good learners just need to get their problem solved). Both need self-reliance, self-confidence, tolerance for uncertainty, resourcefulness, and the disposition to reflect on and to monitor their own thought processes.[21] They need the strategies to fall back on when the routine ways of operating snarl up. The whole apparatus of school, of prescribed knowledge and external evaluation, works against the evolution of these qualities and capabilities. Even many PhDs constitute higher-level trainings rather than the education of ingenious and self-aware minds. There is absolutely nothing wrong with this, provided we are clear what we are and are not getting, and what priority decisions our choice has implicitly committed us to. The only problem, here as before, comes when we try to convince people, or even ourselves, that we are having our cake as well as eating it.

## 'To think straight'

There is a more specific ingredient of the process of science proper, an ability that all scientists need, which lies somewhere between the practical domain of laboratory expertise on the one hand, and the grand world of assumption-busting creativity on the other. It is the ability to think scientifically: to analyse a physical situation, to construct an explanation for how it comes to be the way it is, and then to see what follows, in terms of other physical realities, from the analysis and explanation. It is the ability to see where an idea leads, not just philosophically but empirically, and to see how to check those implications out. Young people are, as we have seen, already somewhat familiar with this ability. They are 'informal' scientists. As a group of science teachers recently noted,

> . . .the learner is already, to some extent, a scientist. The difference between learner and scientist is one of degree rather than kind. They differ in:
> – the care with which they construct hypotheses;
> – the rigour with which they test hypotheses;
> – and the degree to which they can articulate their ideas and understanding.[22]

Scientific thinking exists, in most 11-year-olds, in embryo, we might say. And though it is an ability that is limited in its scope, it makes a very useful tool for the everyday problem solver. It can potentially be disentangled from all the rigmarole of fume cupboards and written reports. It does not always need to involve measurement or computation. It can operate in an intuitive as well as an explicit fashion. It can help you plan a route, choose a new saucepan, redesign the layout of a room, think about where you would like to live, or decide whether this is the year to take that dream holiday. All of these involve creating a description or an explanation of a present state of affairs, and using your knowledge and understanding to extrapolate from them, either in logical thought or in imagination, the consequences of different courses of action.

There is no doubt that the ability to 'think things through' is a useful one, in most jobs and in many areas of life. As a target for science education it avoids the irrelevance to many students of the laboratory skills on the one hand, and the impractical grandiosity of the 'good learner' ideal on the other. The question is: how would science lessons have to change in order to focus on the accomplishment of this objective? And could they change enough, within the surrounding fabric of custom and practice that binds school as we know it together? I shall return to this possibility in the last chapter.

### *'To give students an understanding of the world of science proper'*

We saw in Chapter 4 that the actual process whereby scientific knowledge is generated, accumulated and validated is much less rational and tidy than the popular myth of 'the scientific method' would suggest. Science is a successful creation, not an irrefutable discovery. Ideas spring from irrational sources and tenuous analogies; are defended by career scientists who are often prepared to fight dirty to protect their reputations and promote their ideas; and are checked and validated not by the objective criterion of replicability, but by the informal and often personal judgements of senior members of the scientific sub-culture. At the centre of science we can discern some recurrent methods which rely on the collection of data and the testing of conjectures against evidence, but often they are at least partially obscured by these other factors, which are always more personal and sometimes less creditable.

But what of this human, social, fallible mess do we want all young people to know? From the fact that science proper has been revealed to be like this it does not immediately follow that it has to presented thus, warts and all, in science education. It is possible and valid to study the outlines of history without constantly emphasising the self-interests of its main actors, though it becomes progressively more difficult to ignore them. In the same way it is quite reasonable to start studying the way scientists work, and the way science develops, without dwelling on the motives of individuals or of the community as a whole. In fact there is a continuum one could follow, which runs from a focus on the contents of established scientific belief, through the realisation that these beliefs are human creations – ideas which once were controversial – to the egotistical scramble of *The Double Helix*[23] and the suppression of unwanted results by pseudo-scientific medi-tators, creationists, animal liberationists, nuclear power apologists, civil rights campaigners or multinational drug companies.

What would be the point of educating young people about these realities? Perhaps they should be seen as case studies in the evolution of ideas, interesting in their own right. Science and history teachers could join forces to induct students into the realities of the ways in which cultures develop. Science, recent and remote, does indeed provide some very illuminating examples. Or perhaps we should argue that if science proper *is* so, then we have a moral obligation to inform young people of it; not to do so would be a form of unacceptable censorship and deception. I am less persuaded by this, unless it is put in the context of students developing ability to understand such disillusioning insights; and considered alongside all the other aspects of relative and harsh reality, to which their eyes are gradually opening.

### *'To establish scientific literacy'*

Perhaps a preparation for understanding the nature and status of science proper is to be defended not on intellectual grounds, but more pragmati-cally. It is only by understanding what science is and what it is not, what the realities and pressures are in the scientists' world, that the public can consider the place of that world in society, and therefore be able to take a more informed role in scientific debates. More bluntly, we might argue that people need to be able to protect themselves against being taken in by the claims of scientists to strict objectivity; they should be less susceptible to scientific bullying.

I am inclined to think that this pragmatic type of argument has at least as much force as the more academic forms of justification. In a society that relies so heavily on science to provide for all human needs – heat, light, food, clothing, transportation, medicine, recreation – do not all young people need to know something about the nature of this vast raft of sophistication on which their lives are floating? Yes, clearly they do; but it is not quite so easy to specify what equipment will be of most help. Of course it is useful to have learnt such simple skills as wiring a plug, or using a word processor, though it is not clear whether this needs to happen in school. Most young people seem able to pick up such abilities very quickly at the time they perceive the need for them. And one has to watch carefully that seemingly related subjects of tuition, like building simple electrical circuits or learning the difference between 'compilers' and 'interpreters', are not smuggled in, illicitly, under this rationale. There is an under-standable, though underhand, tendency for teachers to use 'relevance' not as a sufficient end in itself, but as bait to hook students' interest, and then, having caught them, to inveigle them into accepting that academic learn-ing forms a necessary background, or an obvious corollary. You cannot *just* learn how to grow good plants; you usually seem to end up having to go over photosynthesis as well – an understanding that generation after generation of champion gardeners seem to have managed successfully without.

More generally, it would certainly be useful for all young people to be able to communicate with different scientific experts when they needed to. It would be a quite vain hope to suppose that school could equip students to fix their own televisions, or perform their own by-pass oper-ations; but it would be very useful to be able to speak a kind of scientific Esperanto, so that one could ask the engineer or the surgeon sensible questions and evaluate their answers. As with any language, in order to speak it one needs not only skill but confidence, and both of these would need plenty of practice, whether real or simulated, to establish. At the very least, the ability to keep demanding that experts talk to you in a language that you can begin to comprehend is, I would have thought, absolutely vital. Doctors can do it perfectly well if they try.

And more broadly still, people need to be able to speak and understand some science-ese in order to take part, even if only in their own minds, in debates about science-related issues that affect them personally, locally, nationally or globally. We need to be able to spot the difference between science and pseudo-science, or to be able to know when the issue has been obscured so that, without more information, we cannot tell. What are these 'enzymes' they are putting in the washing powder? How can I engage with the issue of whether butter is worse for me than margarine, or vice versa? What *is* the evidence about whether the HIV virus is contained in saliva; or whether homeopathic treatments really work; or whether dyslexia is a real 'disease' or not? What are these 'chemical weapons' we keep hearing about? People get so fed up with not knowing that it is not surprising that they retreat into positions of blind faith, or cling vehemently to scraps of suspect authority gleaned from magazines or consumer affairs programmes. From a value system which says that education is about enabling people to have control over their lives, this aim of directly addressing the issues that are current, and helping people to get a purchase on them, is a very high priority.

Focusing on *contemporary* issues in science is also a better way of giving young people some insight into the nature of scientific inquiry, and the way scientific knowledge develops, than relying on selected topics (like good old Galileo) from history. When we look at historical controversies, we are observing from a vantage point where the outcome seems settled. We cannot now imagine – or it takes a great effort to do so – how people could have been so *stupid* as to have believed in 'caloric' or 'phlogiston' or 'the humours'. Our 20–20 hindsight makes it all look so simple. Yet, at the time, each of these was as fiercely debated, by learned and perceptive people on both sides, as the issues of whether computers can think, or whether intelligence is inherited or innate, are today.

As Harry Collins and Steven Shapin[24] have argued, scientific 'facts' are like ships in bottles, where the bottle represents the judgement of 'truth' by the scientific community. Once a ship is in its bottle, we cannot go back to looking at it as it was when it was unprotected and contentious. It is only by looking at scientific issues that are *currently* controversial that we can see how the battle for acceptance or rejection is fought. And with such contemporary issues, teachers are prevented from retreating into their cosy world of private certainty. They have to join their students in the uncomfortable world of No Right Answer, and in doing so, both teachers and students alike might get a genuine taste of scientific knowledge as the accumulated residue of heated, difficult human conjecture and inquiry. Such issues are also more urgent and important in their own right to students. Now that it is fashionable to be 'green', many of them will genuinely want to know about CFCs and the chemical facts about pollution. It is hard to get worked up about phlogiston.

Here then is a case where we are able, if we wish, to hit a number of educational targets with the same shot. The examination of some currently debated issues, both academic and of social import, is more 'live' to students, and is therefore more likely to engage them better; it forces teachers to adopt a genuinely scientific attitude, rather than an affected one; it shows the uncertain, creative, human side of science; it can provide advice about how to interact with topics that students have a real concern about; and it gives some practice at deciphering and speaking current versions of science-ese.

These then are some of the considerations that might weigh in the balance of deciding what an effective, enjoyable, empowering science education for all young people should look like. In the final chapter I am going to pull together some of the combinations of Possible and Desirable that this chapter has revealed, and work out in a little more detail how a curriculum that is built on them might work. We will need especially to pay attention to the question (long-overdue in this book) of the whole 'life-span' of students' science education, and the way in which emphases might need to change, not only in complexity but in kind, as the time-course of their studies progresses.[25]

## NOTES

[1] See Paul Hirst and Richard Peters, *The Logic of Education*, RKP: London, 1970. C. P. Snow's famous article 'The two cultures' appeared in the *New Statesman*, 6 October 1956.

[2] A detailed exploration of this phenomenon is recorded in F. Marton, D. Hounsell and N. Entwistle, *The Experience of Learning*, Scottish Academic Press: Edinburgh, 1984.

[3] Even arch-critic of education Ivan Illich, in *Deschooling Society*, Penguin: Harmondsworth, 1973 vigorously and unsentimentally defends rote learning as a perfectly valid, and effective, method for accomplishing certain (rather specialised) learning jobs.

[4] Paul Black, personal communication.

[5] Robin Millar (ed.), *Doing Science: Images of Science in science education*, Falmer: London, 1989.

[6] Roger Osborne and Peter Freyberg, *Learning in Science*, Heinemann: Auckland, 1985, pp. 47, 88 and 103.

[7] See Michael Gazzaniga's books *The Social Brain*, Basic Books: New York, 1985, and *Mind Matters*, Houghton Mifflin: Boston, 1988.

[8] Driver, Guesne and Tiberghien, *Children's Ideas in Science, op. cit.*

[9] This distinction was imported into science education by Rosalind Driver and Galen Erickson in an article entitled 'Theories-in-action: some theoretical and empirical issues in the study of students' conceptual frameworks in science', *Studies in Science Education*, 1983, **10**, 37–60.

[10] Paul M. Churchland, *Scientific Realism and The Plasticity of Mind*, CUP: Cambridge, 1979.

[11] Richard White, *Learning Science*, Blackwell: Oxford, 1988.

[12] White was one of the guiding spirits behind the Project to Enhance Effective Learning – the PEEL project – in Melbourne, Australia, described in John Baird and Ian Mitchell (eds), *Improving the Quality of Teaching and Learning*, Monash University Press: Melbourne, Australia, 1986.

[13] See my *Teaching to Learn: A direction for education*, Cassell: London, 1990.

[14] This line of argument was first pursued in my article 'Science Lessens?', *Studies in Science Education*, 1990, **18**, 165–71.

[15] Brian Woolnough and Terry Allsop spell this distinction out very carefully in their *Practical Work in Science*, CUP: Cambridge, 1985.

[16] Michael Young, 'The Schooling of Science ' in Geoff Whitty and Michael Young (eds) *Explorations in the Politics of School Knowledge*, Nefferton Books: Driffield, 1976.

[17] Jane French, 'Accomplishing scientific instruction', in Millar, *op. cit.*

[18] *Science in the National Curriculum*, Department of Education and Science, H.M.S.O.: London, March, 1989.

[19] See for example, Anne Roe, 'A psychological study of eminent psychologists and anthropologists, and a comparison with biological and physical scientists', *Psychological Monographs*, 1953, **67**, No. 2.

[20] Clive Sutton, 'Writing and Reading in Science: The Hidden Messages', in Millar, *op. cit.*

[21] See for a review of creativity, David Perkins, *The Mind's Best Work*, Harvard University Press: Cambridge, Mass., 1981.

[22] Crookes *et al.*, 1985, p.7; quoted by Millar.

[23] James Watson, *The Double Helix*, Weidenfeld and Nicholson: London, 1968.

[24] Harry Collins and Steven Shapin, 'Uncovering the nature of science', *Times Higher Educational Supplement*, 27 July 1984.

[25] Peter Fensham's edited collection *Development and Dilemmas in Science Education*, Falmer: London, 1988 gives several perspectives on the aims of science teaching. Policy statements can be found in *Science for all Americans*, published by the American association for the Advancement of Science, Washington, 1988; and *Science in the National Curriculum*, published by the National Curriculum Council, York, 1988.

# CHAPTER SEVEN

·

# SCIENCE OF THE TIMES

Fingale's First Law: if an experiment works, something has gone wrong.
Fingale's Fourth Law: Once a job is fouled up, anything done to improve it
only makes it worse.

Arthur Bloch

Science education cannot be thought about in a vacuum. It is an expression
of more fundamental educational values, and decisions about its aims and
priorities can only be made relative to those values. Science lessons happen
in schools, and they are therefore contained within a context that itself
represents an educational philosophy. The way science is taught may be
an expression of the values of the school, or it may be at odds with them.
It is up to science teachers to decide the extent to which they are going to
be in the swim of education at large; and whether they are going to be
leading or lagging as far as trends in broad educational thinking are
concerned. If science education is to be got right, its first job is to locate
itself within a more general approach to education.

Up till now, science education has been fundamentally aligned with an
academic, and more recently a vocational, view of education. Science in
the secondary school has revolved around the idea of each unit of study
being a *preparation* for further study or further training, and at the same time
serving to *select* those students who are considered capable of undertaking
the next step. Over the past twenty years or so, as a result of research carried
out within this framework of thought, the quality of science education has
improved significantly for those who, through a combination of aptitude
and inclination, are going to be the successes in this game of educational
Musical Chairs.

But it is not hard to see why, starting from this view of education,
attempts to make science lessons more relevant to the talents, interests and
needs of the majority have consistently failed. The appealing rhetoric of
'process skills', 'real-life problem solving' and 'learning to learn' notwith-
standing, no amount of diluting, gingering up or tinkering with a curricu-

lum that is irredeemably hard and intellectual is going to solve this particular problem. The underlying educational values and practices necessarily reduce such 'curriculum innovation' to mere gestures. It is unclear the extent to which current curriculum reforms around the world address the problem, and arguable that they may yet again compound it. However much you manage to 'lever up standards', an education one of whose main functions is selection is bound to produce as an inevitable waste-product of its search for 'successes' a large pile of relative failures.

Only an education that is actually, and not just rhetorically, founded on the commitment to preparing *all* young people for the challenges they will need to cope with in their later lives, can be defended. Preparation for further study, or kinds of pre-vocational training, do not of themselves constitute such an education. They may well have their place within a mixed portfolio of educational aims; but if they continue to dominate that portfolio, to be its driving force, then the majority of young people are not going to get the education they need and deserve. From this it follows that the familiar form of science education may remain within the secondary curriculum as an option for those whose vocational plans or interests make it appealing. But no variations on the theme will meet the needs of the rest. For them, some model of science education must be created, and implemented, which is going to be of definite use to them in their own lives.

Of course, whatever the curriculum, however relevant, some students will do better at it than others. What is at issue here is not some idealistic notion of 'equality'. The point is that whatever students take away with them should be truly useful in its own right. Vague talk about the traditional curriculum being a general 'training for the mind', and modern waffle about 'real-life problem solving skills', have to be ruthlessly inspected, and if their claims are not clearly substantiated, then the forms of education which they are designed to justify will have to be replaced, downgraded in importance, or converted from Core to Option.

In my own opinion, the paramount purpose of education must be to develop young people's capabilities to live lives that are interesting, fulfilling, self-respecting and kindly. In a settled, structured culture, based on unquestioned values and beliefs, the proper form of such an education might plausibly involve learning the knowledge and *mores* of the culture, and your place within it. But we do not live in such a context. Our culture is typified by uncertainty: personal, social, political and global. Values are, in many of our sub-cultures, weak and conflicting. Information technology is rapidly changing the face of employment. Styles of living and relating are much more varied than they have been, as unfamiliar customs dissolve out into our multi-ethnic world from new arrivals, and traditional cultural bases, especially among the so-called working class, are eroded and collapse. Old churches have lost much of their traditional authority, and in their place we have psychotherapy, cults, evangelism and an influx of religions from other lands.

In the world that young people are going to live in, nothing could be of greater value than the ability to make your own life up as you go along: to find for yourself what is satisfying; to know your own values and your own mind; to meet uncertainty with courage and resourcefulness; and to appraise what others tell you with an intelligent and healthy scepticism. (The *Concise Oxford Dictionary* gives 'sceptical' as 'inclined to suspense of judgement, given to questioning the truth of facts and soundness of inferences'.) Such a frame of mind, sometimes needed by societies only in small quantities, is now a vital commodity for individuals and their cultures alike. Without a willingness to engage with the doubts that surround them, and the resources to do so, people retreat into passivity, superficiality or hostility, stances that militate against one's ability to form fulfilling relationships, work well, amuse oneself harmlessly, and like oneself. The fundamental concern of a useful, contemporary education must be with people's ability to be good learners. Any *other* priority, however cherished, that undermines the commitment to fostering the skilful handling of change, or our success at doing so, will have to be relegated or suspended.

The least we should demand of science education, therefore, is that it does not damage or subvert young people's evolving confidence and expertise as inquirers. Especially we should not allow it to focus on the academic minority if to do so it has to bore, stupefy or intimidate the non-academic majority. If for every student who learns that they *can* 'do science', there have to be three or four who learn that they *cannot*, then that form of education is indefensible. The well-documented status quo, where this is precisely the case, is intolerable, and must be changed with the utmost urgency. Ill-thought-out slogans and injunctions only serve to compound the problem by titillating already frustrated teachers, and confusing students who are enjoined to look for relevance where there is none to be found.

The concern with education as the equipping of all young people with a congenial and well-practised tool-kit for learning is only another slogan, of course, if it does not translate into a more precise set of ideas about both ends and means. We have made a start on this, but it is only a start, and it is the job of each group of specialist teachers, to the extent that they subscribe to it, to clarify the general vision in their own particular area. Science education cannot suddenly turn itself into *the* vehicle for teaching students how to learn: as we have seen, the aim is complex and not yet well-specified enough, and the overall mood of schooling is still in many ways inauspicious. But it can start to see what it can do, in the short term, to offer real relevance without damaging resourcefulness; and in the long term, to design experiences that are demonstrably empowering for all, rather than disabling for many.

A sense of time-scale and priorities is essential if the exercise of deep rethinking is not to generate more good-looking plants with thin and weedy roots, destined to offer more false hope and subsequent disillusion. As well as identifying objectives that are undesirable or incompatible, this planning must mark out those that are for the moment unobtainable, and seek to promote them in different and slower ways. In the light of the greater clarity to which I hope this book has contributed, science education has some hard choices to make. It is because these choices have been largely fudged that teachers are confused and students dissatisfied. The way forward is to specify with much greater clarity what school science is aiming to achieve, and to design the curriculum to meet those aims.

It can seem as if this concern with making distinctions and seeking precision leads one towards a certain view of education, namely that it should proceed by analysing students' needs and the skills that would help them meet those needs down to the nth degree, and then training these, one by one, in a calculated way, as if the learner's intelligence could be assembled bit by bit like a LEGO house. But such a model of education, popular in some quarters at the moment, is not implied by the search for conceptual clarity, and indeed is positively ruled out by the learning analysis I have been developing. The essence of a skill is that one knows intuitively what it is good for and what it is not, and that it is well integrated into one's own way of segmenting and viewing the world. Learning of this type only happens under conditions of personal engagement, responsibility, reflectivity, and the slow accumulation of practice in meaningful situations – and these subjective conditions simply cannot be engineered.[1]

### THE FOUNDATIONS OF GENERAL SCIENCE

The thoughts that follow are meant to be a contribution to the debate about the future of science education, based on the lines of inquiry of the preceding chapters. Let me start by summarising what I think the main lessons of the preceding discussions are.

- Despite much thought, we are still a long way from having a general, useful science education that is a success for all (or even most) young people.
- We cannot teach students simultaneously the accepted views and procedures of science, and the attitudes and strategies of genuine inquiry. If such aims are pursued side-by-side, they must be very clearly distinguished by the teaching medium as well as in its explicit message.

- Education for learning requires time, self-direction and self-evaluation. Better learning skills develop only through first-hand experience that is acquired under those conditions. They must be helped to evolve; such skills cannot be directly grafted on by tuition. At best, training in science proper ignores or suspends this development: it presupposes it. At worst, it ruptures and retards it.
- An education that is based on rote memorisation of abstractions and their associated procedures, or on unmediated confrontations with abstractions too abruptly remote from personal experience to allow disembedding to take place; that confuses exemplification and proof; and that does not allow sufficient time for students to grasp what is going on, will damage rather than consolidate many students' confidence and capabilities as learners.
- There is no evidence that studying the concepts, and learning the procedures, of science proper ever made anybody a better real-life problem solver. There is good reason to suppose that many aspects of the content, material, task demands, social organisation and assessment procedures of science education, as currently conceived, will militate against such transfer. Any rationale for teaching general scientific theories and abstractions (Newton's Laws, kinetic theory of gases, photosynthesis, electromagnetism. . .) that merely *asserts* that such knowledge enhances practical competence, either directly or indirectly, is invalid.
- Emphasising the activities of science proper does not improve students' ability to think scientifically, nor their disposition to do so. It is important to distinguish laboratory skills from cognitive skills.
- Scientific thinking involves an indissoluble trio of aspects: thinking up ideas, thinking them through, and checking them out. In this cycle non-rational processes are as vital as rational and observational. All these need to be educated but cannot be trained. Self-awareness and reflectivity on one's own inquisitive processes are essential adjuncts to scientific thinking.
- Scientific forms of thinking can be developed without any of the paraphernalia of science proper. The acquisition of the concepts and methods of science proper will be made easier and more enjoyable if students already have well-developed habits and skills of scientific thinking.
- Emphasising the *tools* of science proper – precise measurement, mathematics, formal writing, memory for detail – without adequately conveying the *spirit* of scientific inquiry is educationally inept: it either turns students off, or it leaves them tooled-up but dependent on instruction for tool *use*.
- Informal topics and non-technical methods can stretch and educate the academically-inclined as well as the less intellectual students. Concern

about 'holding back the bright' cannot be used as an argument for retaining any concepts, topics or methods of science proper in parts of the curriculum with which all students are required to struggle.

- Working knowledge – that which informs spontaneous learning – is different from intellectual knowledge. Thought serves as a practical guide to action only if a) it has crystallised out of first-hand experience, and remains tied to it; or b) taught formulations have, through *additional* experience, been allowed to dissolve back into the level of intuition.
- Young people are in a sense 'scientists', but their scientific thinking is often careless, sporadic, value-laden, intuitive and situation-specific. However the skills and aims of scientists are crucially different from those which students might find useful in everyday life. Whilst there is a class of real-life problems where people's thinking would undoubtedly benefit from greater precision, there is no universal value in accuracy and quantification, or articulation and justification, for their own sakes. Real-life learning is often fine when it is intuitive and approximate.
- Those many students for whom studying science has been a predominantly negative experience will be prone to feel powerless and uninterested in science-related issues subsequently.
- Science involves irrational and social pressures, as well as rational thinking. Scientific knowledge is a human creation, not a store of discovered truth. It is preferable for students to discover these attributes by analysing current controversies, both academic and those with social implications, than by looking down the inverted telescope of history.
- It is of great value, in our society, for young people to be able to speak and understand some science-ese (for talking to repair people, especially doctors), and to be intuitively alert for the misuse of the jargon or appurtenances of science proper to boost sales pitches, knowledge claims or personal and corporate status. It is impossible to teach them enough at school to make them experts in any field. It should be possible to give them the confidence to ask pertinent questions, and to detect rubbish in the answers.
- Science education should be able to provide, and help young people discuss, the best knowledge available about science-related issues of general social or global concern.
- If science teachers want to develop positive attitudes towards science proper in students, it should be a routine and continual part of their job to model enthusiastic and voluntary engagement with scientific problems, both by visible involvement with their own projects, and by being visibly inquisitive and well-informed about topical scientific issues, both theoretical and practical/social.

A FRAMEWORK FOR EFFECTIVE SCIENCE EDUCATION

On these foundations I now wish to erect a framework for science education. As throughout the book, I shall have only a little to say about primary, post-compulsory, and informal education; my main focus will be on science education in secondary schools. Some of what I shall advocate is already common practice. Some is enshrined in current curriculum innovation – though its impact remains to be seen. Some is happening in a few schools to a greater or lesser extent, and in a more or less experimental fashion. And some will be beyond the bounds of what is currently practicable, except in unusually friendly conditions. I am very far from claiming that everything I think should happen is brand new, or that it should somehow be realisable by all hard-pressed teachers working in today's schools. Rather I hope to show how initiatives which are sometimes of a piecemeal or tentative nature can be drawn together and underpinned by a coherent, powerful and explicit rationale – the one which has slowly emerged from the discussions in this book.

In a sense this last chapter is the least important in the book. I believe that the most important conditions for change are an uncompromising perception that change is needed, and an analysis of the situation that makes sense of those perceptions, and at the same time offers some general vision or direction for improvement. Without these, there is neither the will nor the confidence to engage fully with the debate about how that vision is to be instantiated. When people are engaged in such a committed debate, ideas and experiments are bound to be generated, taken seriously, and taken on their merits. Without commitment, any idea, however good, can be shot down or ignored, especially those that originate from 'outsiders'. My intention here has been to mount another challenge – one that I hope has been both unflinching and positive – to an aspect of education that is insupportable, and which most of its practitioners know to be so, in order that the necessary sense of urgency be fomented. I want the questions and directions to remain when the half-baked answers I am about to describe have been rejected or superseded. So I apologise to readers who have been waiting for the detailed diagnosis to be followed by a definitive prescription: you are going to be disappointed. But I reject entirely the cynic's charge that criticism is only to be taken seriously if the critic can generate watertight answers to his or her own points. Chapters 1 to 6 will not go away however many holes are shot in Chapter 7.

*Primary science*

It is vital that the long tentacles of the traditional induction into science proper do not reach down and twist what happens in the name of science in primary schools. The proper words for things, the proper way of measuring things, the proper format for writing things up – all these are premature, potentially intimidating and deadening, if imposed at this stage. They should not be introduced unless, as occasionally happens, the children positively clamour for them, and if they subsequently forget or misuse them, they should not be corrected or reminded. If a jam-jar will do, then that is what they will get. (And if they use a jam-jar and *discover* that it will not do, then so much the better.) If they run up against problems of 'fair testing' or precise measurement, the last thing the teacher should do is solve them for them. Grappling with such problems is of the essence of science, and ingenuity is only developed in the struggle. Worries about 'blind alleys' and 'reinventing the wheel' are inappropriate. Children learn as much from ventures that fail as they do from those that deliver what was expected – provided the adults around them don't react to failure as 'failure'. And when the emphasis is on strengthening the powers of invention, not the production of wheels, it does not matter how many other people have tackled the problem before, nor the quality of their solutions.

Their study should be built around the slowly gathering sophistication of three simple questions: How Come?, So What? and What If? These sum up the three processes of creative puzzlement, drawing out implications, and testing ideas through observation, which are at the heart of scientific thinking, both formal and informal. Their activities should involve chatting, looking for patterns, and messing about with dud toasters, woodlice or mustard-and-cress 'to see what happens if. . .'. How come a metal bar sinks but a metal tray floats? What about a pin? The severed lid of a can? What if we use soapy water?

They do not need test-tubes, and should be encouraged to undertake experiments whose products they can eat.[2] Science should be muddled up with creative writing, and children should start to keep a private notebook, as scruffy and undisciplined as they like, of things that intrigue them, funny observations, and vague ideas. Regularly children should be invited to contribute from this source ideas that could go into a class 'register of research' – a bank of projects to be added to, drawn upon, and incorporated by responsive teachers into their teaching schemes.

## Science 11–14

In the early years of secondary school, science teaching should be divided into four themes or strands, clearly demarcated from each other. The first is the *inquiry theme*, in which the project-centred approach of the primary school is continued and deepened. Students work individually or in small groups (as they prefer) on projects of their own choice, under the supervision of the teacher – or of older students in the school, who would gain

valuable experience from the role. Here are two examples of possible
projects, the first suitable for the younger, and the second for the older,
end of this age range:

A class carried out an investigation into the gassing of badgers to prevent the
spread of bovine tuberculosis among dairy cattle and infection of humans. Pupils
themselves raised the issue during class discussion and planned all aspects of the
inquiry. The project enabled them to clarify their own views on the issue, to
find out about other points of view and to suggest possible plans of action.

Pupils collected information on different aspects of the issue from books and
newspapers. Through the local newspaper they invited people to tell them
about badgers' setts in the area. With the help of an expert they investigated
badger signs, tracks and holes in the school woods. Letters were sent to various
organisations (Ministry of Agriculture, conservation societies, television programmes and the police) to express their concerns and to find out more
information about badgers. A questionnaire was designed and sent to different
local schools to find out about other children's perceptions of the issue. Pupils
identified the arguments for and against the gassing of badgers.

This example illustrates how controversial issues relating to the environment
can be introduced to children to encourage in them an awareness and motivation for action. The use of an action-based approach may stimulate them to
form their own judgement in the light of evidence.

In one locality, links were established between British and Norwegian
secondary schools in order to do some collaborative work on the issue of acid
rain. For a year the pupils carried out analyses of water pollutants and acid
precipitation in their own environment. They were able to exchange their
experiences and findings with their linked class.

The survey involved analysis of the acidity of precipitation and lake water,
plus analysis of the buffering effect of different rocks and recording of weather
conditions. The results were displayed in the form of graphs with the use of
microcomputers, and the findings were exchanged between schools in the two
countries through letters and videos.

To interpret the results from both countries, the pupils looked for background information from various sources. Statutory and voluntary organisations
provided videos, slides, pamphlets and official statements, offering contrasting
views on the issue. Scientists from government associations came to discuss the
scientific aspects of acid rain. Representatives from the Norwegian Embassy
and non-government bodies added an important political and social dimension.

The pupils communicated their views and findings through a range of media
– newspapers, radio and television.[3]

Groups would present progress reports to the class as a whole on a rotating
basis. In consultation with the supervisor, projects should be capable of
being modified or even abandoned as work on them proceeds. A central
role for the supervisor at this stage would be the encouragement of
students' reflection on the *process* of inquiry, so that their ability to monitor
and evaluate their strategies, in the light of events, becomes an habitual
resource. 'What are we doing?', 'How is it going?', and 'What else could
we try?' would be typical of the kinds of reflective questions that students
learn to spend time dwelling on as a matter of course. Students should

become used to planning investigations, as well as carrying them out. They should be allowed to start work on problems that involve questions of value and ethics, or those for which scientific approaches turn out to be inappropriate, so that they develop the essential feel for the scope and limitations of scientific thinking, and for the place it has within more complex kinds of problem solving.

As in primary school, the class should spend time developing its own stockpile of topics for investigation. Teachers may add topics of their own to this pile, but not ones which are drawn from the disembodied world of science proper, nor to the extent that their contributions threaten to dominate the list. They may not offer any technical equipment, concepts or vocabulary unless it is demanded, and then only in a tentative and flexible spirit. (Sex education should certainly not be introduced in a quasi-scientific manner.) Their role is much more one of gentle questioning of students' formulations and 'conclusions', so that the students themselves are led towards a perception of the usefulness of precision in both thought and observation. Teachers will have to develop the habit of attentive listening, so that they can always talk to students in terms of the ideas that they, the students, are already using. Private writing and informal discussion should still be encouraged, but groups of students should be asked to write accounts of their projects for other groups to read. In this way they will again come to see for themselves why explicit, detailed and well-articulated writing is a necessary part of the scientists' skill.

The second theme, I suggest, is an extension of the primary school experience of taking things to bits called the *how it works* theme. Teachers can build up stores of bits of technology, or examples of natural, everyday processes, of varying degrees of complexity for students to try to figure out. Items of discarded kitchen equipment, simple engines and motors, radios and record-players, even televisions would provide suitable material, as would the behaviour of yeasts in breadmaking, or of different bacteria in cheesemaking. This theme would require close collaboration between science and design and technology teachers – a distinction that anyway makes more sense to planners than it does to students. In the course of these investigations, teachers would be able to offer some ways of describing and explaining how things work, but would be restrained from using these discussions as stalking-horses, under cover of which to start 'teaching' about Ohm's Law or cellular structure. They should themselves learn, and therefore be able to convey, the fact that a good explanation is relative to the purposes and understandings of the inquirer, and that at every level there are going to be questions left unanswered.

The third theme aims at developing the *critical consumer* in students. Advertisements should be routinely scrutinised for bogus science, or for those that play on the presumed ignorance or gullibility of consumers. Those targeted at teenagers should be a special source of interest. A rolling class project should write letters to manufacturers about claims for their products with requests for access to the evidence on which those claims are based; and should involve the Advertising Standards Authority and consumer watchdog organisations and media programmes. Groups of students should conduct their own 'Which?' reports into various goods and products, and should send the results to manufacturers with requests for comments. Issues of particular local concern would be most interesting to pursue. In collaboration with English and Humanities teachers, students could set up their own advertising agencies, and work on producing copy that is alternatively designed to either bamboozle or enlighten other students.

Other presentations of science in the media should also be monitored, with a special eye kept on the unspoken assumptions or values that they contain. What message about life-styles and the value of 'labour-saving devices' is conveyed by the plethora of gadgets paraded before the viewers of *Tomorrow's World*? What view of human beings' relation to the animal world lies behind particular wild-life programmes? How rational are different attitudes to different types of animals: contrast current depictions of rats and cats, cockroaches and ladybirds, seals and sharks, gorillas and hyenas, flies and butterflies, cows and calves, for example.

The final theme in this age range is a *study* theme. This is the only time when teachers are able to transmit scientific knowledge, and topics should be chosen so that they are likely to engage the vast majority of students. In general the selection of topics should be guided by the following four criteria:

1. They are of direct, immediate use to students in understanding and interacting with their everyday environment, about which they do not already have adequate working knowledge, and students agree that this is so when it is explained. OR
2. They are of indirect use, in that there is clear and incontrovertible evidence that studying or investigating them will result in the emergence of skills, understandings or awareness that are of direct, immediate use, and which students do not already possess. OR
3. They are overwhelmingly agreed by the community of science teachers to be necessary objects of study, despite their lack of demonstrated utility. OR
4. They are overwhelmingly agreed by the students to be intrinsically interesting.

These criteria mean that certain familiar topics of the secondary science curriculum may no longer form elements of compulsory study for the

11–14 age group, unless the students overwhelmingly request them. They include photosynthesis, statistical and molecular genetics, the kinetic theory of gases, the particulate theory of matter, the periodic table and allied concepts such as reactivity and chemical bonding, force, energy and electromagnetism. These clearly fail to meet criteria 1 and 2, and I am confident that they would also fail 3. The criteria also mean that certain familiar mainstays of laboratory procedure cannot be 'taught' unless they are demanded by the students.

A central theme, one which meets these criteria better than most, is that of human biology, and it should be given considerable weight during this period. Topics covered should be basic anatomy and physiology; a particular focus on the psychophysiology of the special senses (interpreted to mean not exclusively vision, and including plenty of investigations of perceptual thresholds and discriminations, illusions etc.); the central nervous system and the rudiments of brain structure and function; life-span development from conception to death; human evolution, from both biological and cultural perspectives. There should be lively presentations of the bones of these 'stories', without much jargon, but with some examination of the evidence on which knowledge claims have been based. The exhibitions in the Hall of Human Biology at the Natural History Museum in London, or the Exploratorium in San Francisco, and quality TV series such as those of David Attenborough, provide a good indication of the tone and level that should be aimed for here.

Issues of basic health and lifestyle, and informal medical techniques could be linked in: students might carry out investigations or surveys on the relative efficacy of various types of pain-killers, homeopathic remedies, cures for the common cold, approaches to childbirth, the effect of diet on mood and mood on diet, influences on bowel movements and so on. Can people predict or control their own temperatures? How hard is it to change habits, and what conditions make it easier to? A perennial topic should be the learning habits, styles and processes of members of the class: each class should be constantly monitoring its own way of learning, so that self-awareness in this vital area is developed, and individual differences revealed. There are hundreds of investigations that can be done using yourself as the object of study. Such inquiries would further practice the skills of objectivity, while having the beneficial side-effect of raising students' awareness of, and sense of responsibility for, their own physical health. The temptation to preach and moralise should be avoided, on the obvious grounds that a significant proportion of adolescents are learning how to assert themselves against adult power, and that opposition is, during that stage, a higher priority for them than the evaluation of advice.

SCIENCE 14–16

Beyond the age of 14, or the point where preferences are expressed, and the first steps on career paths are taken, science education should split into two parts, one compulsory and one optional. The compulsory part should again contain several strands. Project work should continue, but should be allowed (but not required) to move in the direction of science proper – i.e. it may now be based on laboratory tests and derive from an existing scientific framework. A degree of choice should remain in the selection of such projects, collaboration in carrying them out should still be encouraged, though reports should be written individually, and assessment should be based on the quality of the reflective process rather than the tidiness of the outcome. Likewise the study of how things work should persist, but students should be encouraged to research for themselves the underlying principles that are involved in their chosen piece of technology, and should take turns in presenting their explanations to the class as a whole.

Other project-type themes might involve talking to experts, where students make an acceptable nuisance of themselves by button-holing people who work with science or technology and quiz them about the knowledge they use. Local GPs, science teachers in higher and further education, scientists and engineers in local industries, photocopying machine and television repair people, laboratory technicians, pharmacists, builders, surveyors and electricians, nurses and ambulance workers. . .all these and many others would be prime targets. The object of the exercise is for students to develop the knowledge and the confidence required to discuss science-related areas in which they are not experts with people who are – an invaluable asset in our technological society, as we have seen. They should learn to listen carefully, and would be repeatedly feeding back their gathering understanding to their informants, using phrases like 'Well, would it be fair to say, then. . .?'; 'If I've got you right, that means. . .'; and 'OK, but how do you go about . . .?'Older students pursing specialist science studies should be constantly being called upon by 14-year-olds to talk about what they are currently learning – an interaction that would benefit the older at least as much as the younger.

There should be a more didactic theme looking at current controversies in science, which could have some 'set pieces', but should also be flexible enough to capitalise on issues as they emerge. It is just not true that people have to plough through years of the 'old' school science before they are capable of getting some sort of a purchase on such topical issues. The real, technical science that lies behind space satellites, test-tube babies or genetic engineering is far too difficult for even 'A level' students to grasp from first principles, yet most people could quite quickly get a rough idea of what the major scientific problems involved are, and the general form of the solutions. Being able to recite the halogen gases, or to measure the length of a standing sound wave, is not really going to be much of a help in such situations. It is possible to learn a lot of science by jumping in the deep end – and it tends to be much more interesting than constantly doing 'practicals' that are to the young scientist like an endless diet of scales would be to a budding pianist. Also, as I argued before, students at this age are ready to be given a feel for the competitive, tendentious, faltering process whereby scientific knowledge is generated and scrutinised; and this is much better done by looking at current claims and controversies than by trying to put back the uncertainty into historical disputes which are now cut and dried.

What could students study? Some possible issues would be the origin of the universe, as discussed by Stephen Hawking in *A Brief History of Time*; the evolution of intelligence, as proposed, for example, by Julian Jaynes in *The Origin of Consciousness in the Breakdown of the Bicameral Mind*, and Richard Passingham in *The Human Primate*; James Lovelock's 'Gaia hypothesis', which proposes that the whole biosphere functions like a living organism to regulate its own constitution, outlined in his book *Gaia: A New Look at Life on Earth* and popularised by Peter Russell in *The Awakening Earth*; Rupert Sheldrake's very controversial theory of 'morphic resonance', which argues that learning can propagate between different groups of animals without them having any contact with each other (see his *A New Science of Life*); or new ideas about the function of the brain, such as those of Michael Gazzaniga (*Mind Matters*) or Marvin Minsky (*The Society of Mind*).[4]

All these positions are not proven at the moment, nor are they likely to be finally accepted or rejected for a while. But the point is not whether they are 'right' or not, but that they are living examples of the cutting edge of science, with all its personalities, vested interests and doubts. Every 14-year-old in the country should have been following the 'cold fusion' controversy as it unfolded, and should be set *Horizon* as regular homework. Science teachers do not have to be experts on every such topic, anxious lest they are asked a question to which they do not yet know the answer. All they have to do is be interested, along with the students, in what is going on, and to have some ideas about how to find out more on topics that grab the interest of the class.

As well as keeping abreast of theoretical issues, it should be a prominent theme at this age to keep abreast of some of the social issues in science. Like much else that I am advocating, this is already part of common practice, or at least common rhetoric. The National Curriculum for science in England and Wales, for example, mentions all of the following issues: farming (fertilisers, cloning, factory methods and the over-culling of resources such as fish); drugs; malnutrition and starvation; AIDS and medicine; expensive life-support technology (pacemakers, kidney machines, incubators); genetic engineering; pollution (water purity, acid rain, the ozone layer, the 'greenhouse' effect, noise pollution); fossil fuels (lead in petrol, petrochemical industry); information technology; non-renewable and alternative energy sources (including nuclear power); space travel. And there are many others that one could add. To have some working knowledge of the science that is involved in such issues, and of the pros and cons of different methods for researching them, as well as of the competing claims that are made, would seem to be one of the bare necessities for a scientifically literate, and therefore possibly scientifically responsible, society.

As an extension of earlier work on the human body and mind, I suggest a special study theme at this age that focuses on topics in medical research – AIDS, cancer, heart disease, premature baby care, contraception, fertility drugs, transplants, neurological disorders and approaches to mental 'illness' (such as schizophrenia and depression) that rely on psychotherapeutic as well as psychopharmacological perspectives. (The understanding of mental health is scandalously ignored, even by current approaches to health education.) These again provide topical and personally relevant examples through which students' understanding of the value, limitations and methods of science proper can be gradually deepened.

All students must follow this 'core'; if the 'bright' ones are allowed to take courses in 'science proper' instead, then, as has happened many times already in the attempt to provide a useful education for the non-academic students, the core will become seen as second-rate, and will not command the respect of either teachers or students. However, something that looks more like school science as we currently know it should be available as an option for students to take if they want to, or need to. In this 'topics in routine science' course, teachers would be able to teach some of the areas that had been prohibited to them elsewhere, and especially to introduce more of the conventional frameworks of physics, chemistry and biology. The emphasis here is clearly on mastery rather than discovery, and students will work in an environment where there are definitely right understandings and good experiments. This is the place where pre-vocational aims, and preparation for further study, can be pursued without having to pretend that students are also 'finding things out' in any very important sense. They have started their apprenticeship in the world of science proper, and like all apprentices, their first job, before there can be any thought of creativity, is to master the knowledge, language, skills and mores of the craft. And as in most apprenticeships, students should also be required to know something of the history of the guild which they have chosen to join. Here is the place to study some of the formative points in the development of science as we now know it, so that the concepts that are being learnt seem less *ex cathedra*, and more grounded and motivated within a continuous process of intellectual evolution.

This sort of learning will be made much more easy and enjoyable as a result of a firm intuitive grounding in scientific thinking. Students will have a much clearer sense of what is going on and why in the world of science proper if they have first gained some confidence with the rudiments of scientific forms of thought in informal, everyday, contexts. There is no evidence that the kind of understanding of science that is typically achieved by a successful school-leaver requires a lengthy induction into science proper over many years. On the contrary, as Peter Fensham, an Australian science educator, puts it, 'there appears to be no inherent need to spend four, six or eight years of slow build-up of this sort of scientific knowledge.'[5] The insistence on feeding watered-down versions of the academic curriculum to younger students, and to the whole range of students, seems to reflect a lack of imagination about what else to do, and a reluctance to let the trusty content go, more than a principled position. Time would be better spent, for scientifically-minded students as well as the others, mastering the scope and limitations of informal scientific thinking, and learning some relevant ideas about the modern world. It would be more interesting, and it would stand them in better stead for both 'real life' *and* further study of science proper.

## SCIENCE BEYOND 16

After the point at which compulsory education ends, some strand of general, non-technical education in science should probably be continued, even up to university. The activities of the 14–16 core science course could easily be extended to cover more topics, and to respond opportunistically to current events. The technical courses of 'A level' and undergraduate science are themselves narrowly focused on the acquisition of correct factual knowledge, theoretical understanding and laboratory skill. Students disappear into the minutiae of each subject very rapidly, and are often not given the time or encouragement to develop a more synoptic, let alone a critical, view of the field. Both the social and the reflective dimensions of science education are frequently missing from post-compulsory study for science students, just as they are for non-scientists; and it would be in the interests of the general good for both groups to develop a broader sense of the strengths and weaknesses of science.

### THE CONDITIONS FOR CHANGE

As I said earlier, I consider the ideas in the preceding section merely a sketch that might stimulate some discussion, not a well-formed proposal that I have any interest in defending. It is up to science teachers to see if it rings any bells; if it seems to capture something of their experience and their ideals. No book could do much to address the state of stress that many teachers are experiencing. But some accessible ideas that are not just fine-sounding, but which seem to offer practical avenues for progress, both at the level of individual teachers' classroom activities, and as fodder for discussion, might provide the basis of some much-needed control and a cautious seed of optimism. If what I have said is intelligible, plausible and at least potentially fruitful, then the next stage is to see how it can be sharpened and converted into a programme of things to try out, think through and campaign for.

I am more and more convinced that the only people who can plan, initiate and carry through the kind of change of educational emphasis that is required are teachers themselves.[6] There are three reasons for believing this. First, teaching is a profession, and teachers are jealous of their tenuous prerogative to be the architects of education as well as its deliverers. Second, they have the experience of what schools and schoolchildren are actually like on which to base assessments of what needs to, and can, be done. And third, they have it in their professional power to subvert, ignore or neutralise any innovation which is foisted on them, and which they either do not like, or have not been given enough time to implement successfully. The changes brought into being by recent curriculum innovation around the world have caused a tremendous amount of kerfuffle for the teachers, and may well have minimal effect on the quality of education received by the students. If the *real* revolution is to happen, it has to happen first in the hearts and minds of thousands of individual teachers.

Teachers will not be able to undertake this quest, though, if they do not have congenial conditions and adequate support, or are not in the right frame of mind for it. If they are feeling stressed, trapped and attacked they will deny their own doubts and ideals, and dedicate their energies to resisting impositions and protecting their own well-being as best they can. The main prerequisites for educational change, therefore, are teachers' willingness to engage with the issues, and a sense of honesty, solidarity and intellectual openness in the pursuit and appraisal of suggestions. Teachers at the moment are in great need of exactly those resources and attitudes of 'the good learner' that we have just touched upon. Resignation, entrenchment, cynicism and depression are symptoms of the disengaged; understandable though these stances are, they do neither individual teachers, nor schools, nor education as a whole, any good in the long run. If reform is going to happen that is more than mere gestures, teachers need to be involved with it from the word go, and they need to be on good form.

So what shape are teachers in? Is the climate congenial for self-initiated change? I think it is not yet, but the signs are positive that it could be, once the headaches and teething troubles of imposed change have settled down. There is no doubt, for example, that science teachers are full of concerns about the overall value of what they are doing, and realistically sceptical about the lack of impact that the current reforms are going to have. Most secondary science teachers, I am certain, know that there are large numbers of their students for whom learning science is neither an enjoyable nor an enriching experience. They know that much of it is difficult, out-of-date, remote and unhelpful. Some of these are busy experimenting with their teaching, and are devising courses and approaches that offer something better. But many feel stuck. They do not have a clear idea of what a science education that would work for everyone would look like. They hear the rhetoric of educationalists about the potential of science to be a valuable preparation for real-life learning and thinking, and find it congenial, or even inspiring. But they remain saddled with an expanding array of topics to be 'covered', assessments to be made, and with an entire infrastructure of books, equipment and expectations that drag them back into the dubious traditional channels of orthodox experiments and explanations.

These doubts and questions are offset for many science teachers by a more general belief in the worthwhile-ness of what they do. Despite the moments when teachers are aware that the ground on which they stand is precarious, that when they try to plant their feet firmly, they cannot find a solid bottom to their own understanding, nevertheless they will feel that much of the time they are competent professionals. Though they cannot quite tailor their science so that it appeals to all, they retain their faith in the value of scientific skills and, more broadly, the 'scientific method'. So science teachers frequently experience both confidence and insecurity about their work – an ambivalence that is characteristic of the teaching profession more widely. It seems quite normal to be somewhat hypocriti-cal: both feeling dissatisfied with one's existing way of working *and* clinging to that way in the face of the uncertainties and demands of change.

Part of their reluctance to let go of the traditional formulations of school science is that science teachers themselves feel comfortable with, and like, the world they create. Whether or not science education pays off for all students in terms of real-life competence, it is a domain of learning that poses its own internal problems, and offers its own rewards, and science teachers have, for whatever reasons, derived satisfaction from engaging with it. What's more, all secondary science teachers have been successful at learning science in the conventional way – by definition, being graduates in a scientific subject – and have, for the most part, enjoyed their scientific studies. The challenges to grasp a new principle, to begin to see a pattern of behaviour in a collection of results, to do a clean experiment, have been on the whole manageable, and have given them pleasure and self-confidence.

One of their intentions as teachers is to enable others to gain access to science (thus construed), and to have a similarly fruitful time grappling with it. The regret and self-doubt that they experience as they see many students failing to do so is compensated for by the others, perhaps only a minority, who do begin to catch on. They strongly resist the conclusion that academic science (like every other field of study) is something that has intrinsic appeal for only a minority of young people – the minority that they themselves belonged to. To justify their own enthusiasm, they keep asserting that what they *enjoyed* is good for all, and that if it fails to excite large numbers of young people, then there is something wrong somewhere – with the syllabus, with the kids, or even with themselves.

Peter Fensham sums up this problem thus:

> Historically, only a relatively small percentage of a population have [sic] been fascinated by scientific knowledge for its own sake. . .two of the things that mark off many science teachers, scientists and most science curriculum developers from the great majority of their peers are their interest in scientific knowledge as such and their willingness to persist in its learning. It is neither surprising nor unnatural that persons educated extensively in science should look at the world, and at schooling, through eyes that are conditioned by scientific knowledge. This, however, means that what they see as important, significant and worthy of learning is likely to be different from what persons uneducated in science see when they look to science as a phenomenon in their lives and in society. For example. . .those educated in science give a priority to precise definition and explanations while others are more interested in information and how to apply it.
>
> Science educators, part of the educated in science, have tended to set out to create science education for schools that mirror [sic] their own (and science's) priorities. Hence the emphasis on conceptual knowledge and on the intellectual processes that are used with, and in the generation of, this sort of knowledge. . .By and large, and with very few exceptions, the science curriculum projects of the '60s and '70s set out to extend science as it was known in the curriculum of elite secondary schooling to a much wider cross-section of school learners. In other words, the content and topics of these elite science curricula were taken as the knowledge of science that was worth learning more generally, and the projects devoted their energies to devising new presentations and forms of pedagogy which it was hoped would achieve this goal. . . If we are to progress with Science for All, it may well be necessary to reverse this process radically.[7]

The rhetoric of 'process science' seemed to many science teachers to offer a way out of their ambivalence. With an increased emphasis on science as an activity, as a potentially powerful and reliable way of finding things out and solving problems, and a relegation of the traditionally difficult concepts to a somewhat less central place, science education should have become both a more useful training of the mind, and more accessible to all students, regardless of their academic aptitudes or career aspirations. Process science seemed to hold out the possibility that induction into the world of scientific practice, and the expansion of informal skills of investigation and problem solving, can be achieved side by side. With enough ingenuity in designing the science curriculum – both as topics and methods of teaching – we should have been able to resolve the tension without having to give up the periodic table and photosynthesis, titration and dissection.

So there is an understandable reluctance to accept, despite all the evidence of the last twenty years, that this dual approach is not going to solve their problems. Generations of the less academic students have failed to be turned on by a series of much-vaunted innovations. Still sympathetic in principle to any approach that emphasises skills, processes, and relevance, older teachers at least are wary of becoming too enamoured, remembering that the 'guided discovery' approaches of Nuffield and Chemstudy in the 60s, which were meant to achieve exactly the same liberation, have turned out to be the orthodoxy of the 1980s from which they are now trying, again, to escape. Likewise I suspect that many science teachers have greeted the new 'attainment targets', in the National Science Curriculum for England and Wales, of 'Exploration of Science' and 'The Nature of Science' with the same mixture of sympathy and scepticism, afraid that it is new wine in old bottles, and *'plus ça change, plus c'est la même chose'*. An unhappy history of naive optimism tends to leave fatalism as its residue, and this militates, unfortunately, against teachers' feeling like getting stuck in once more.

Yet it is science teachers' desire to have their cake and eat it that has effectively neutralised many attempts to broaden the relevance and appeal of school science, from Nuffield onwards. For it has turned out that the concepts and methods of laboratory science are 'dominant', in the geneticist's sense; any hybrid curriculum inevitably, and usually rapidly, reverts to something that is at best a minor variation on the traditional theme, and the introduced strain of 'inquiry' or 'open-endedness' is effectively subverted. Curriculum developers and science educationalists, whose job it is think their way through such dilemmas clearly and realistically, have been largely to blame for encouraging science teachers in this vain hope. They have touted 'science – a process approach' and 'open-ended investigations' without seeing that the left-hand of the residual content is constantly going to pull the rug out from under the right-hand of proclaimed inquiry. And teachers have become more bamboozled than ever as a result.

A New Zealand ex-teacher, W.J. Fletcher, not a science teacher, but with a keen interest in science, was asked about ten years ago to address the national science teachers' association. He did not mince his words. He said:

> I am going to make some accusations about science teachers and science teaching. First I accuse you science teachers of devoting your energies to the mere conveying of scientific knowledge and principles – to being, in other words, animated textbooks. . .to the point where your pupils think that that's all science is. . .
>
> Secondly I accuse you of giving your pupils a false idea of the essence of science. . .I accuse you of not conveying the great truth that the essence of science is a method – a messy, imaginative, often unsystematic business in which luck and persistence play a great part. . .I accuse you under this charge of conveying to your pupils the false idea that the models and analogies you use for explaining scientific ideas are exact representations of what actually is, rather than being, as they are, imaginative constructions of the human mind.
>
> My third accusation is that you haven't done much to help your average and below-average pupils to distinguish science from non-science. . . .[8]

Let me just voice the guess that many science teachers in 1990, if they had not been put on the back foot by being attacked by outsiders, would very largely agree. Yes, they would say, but show us how. Show us how we can explain what we want to do to the articulate parents of potential physicists. Show us how we can run our classes in a different way while keeping all our students safe. Show us how we can make 'forces' come alive. Show us how we can avoid lessons degenerating into chaos if we give a significant weight of responsibility to students who expect to be controlled. Show us how we can do all this while keeping our exam passes respectable. Show us how we can assess – and therefore defend – a curriculum that is truly based on exploration. Go on, show us. I cannot claim to have convincing answers to such specific and important questions – but I *am* convinced that answers that are truly satisfactory will only emerge as a result of vigorous and radical debate amongst science teachers themselves – a process to which those like myself who have the leisure to research and develop ideas can contribute, but which we should not seek to hijack or preempt.

## NOTES

[1] See Margaret Carr and Guy Claxton, 'The costs of calculation', *New Zealand Journal of Educational Studies*, 1989, **24**, 129–40.

[2] See Vicki Cobb, *Science Experiments You Can Eat*, Lippincott: New York, 1972.

[3] Quoted from 'Environmental education', Curriculum Guidance 7, National Curriculum Council, York, 1990.

[4] Stephen Hawking, *A Brief History of Time*, Bantam: Toronto, 1988; Julian Jaynes, *The Origin of Consciousness in the Breakdown of the Bicameral Mind*, Houghton Mifflin: Boston, 1976; Richard Passingham, *The Human Primate*, W. H. Freeman: Oxford,

1982; James Lovelock, *Gaia: A New Look at Life on Earth*, OUP: Oxford, 1979; Peter Russell, *The Awakening Earth*, Ark: London, 1984; Rupert Sheldrake, *A New Science of Life*,Anthony Blond: London, 1985; Michael Gazzaniga, *Mind Matters*, Houghton Mifflin: Boston, 1988; Marvin Minsky, *The Society of Mind*, Picador: London, 1987.

[5] Peter Fensham, 'Science for all: a reflective essay', *Journal of Curriculum Studies*, 1985, **17**, 415–35. This article represents the published position that is perhaps the closest to the one I am developing here concerning the adolescent science curriculum.

[6] These ideas concerning teachers and innovation are spelled out in my *Being a Teacher: A Positive Approach to Change and Stress*, Cassell: London, 1989.

[7] Fensham, *op. cit.*

[8] W. J. Fletcher, 'Science teaching: are we nurturing scientists or conformists?', *New Zealand Science Teacher*, 1979, **21**, 46–54.

# INDEX